ART FOR EVERYDAY

ART FOR EVERYDAY

BY PATRICIA CONWAY

Principal Photography by Jon Jensen
Design by Elizabeth Van Itallie
Special Assistance by Dominique Lalli

Clarkson Potter/Publishers
New York

THE NEW CRAFT MOVEMENT

To Roger, Justin, and Alexander

Also by Patricia Conway
*Ornamentalism: The New Decorativeness
in Architecture and Design* (with Robert Jensen)

Endpapers: William Morris Willow Wallpaper, 1874 from *William Morris:
Designs and Patterns* by Norah Gillow. Courtesy Crescent Books

Photograph credits appear on page 264.

Copyright © 1990 by Patricia Conway
Photographs copyright © 1990 by Jon Jensen
All rights reserved. No part of this book may be reproduced or transmitted in any form or by any
means, electronic or mechanical, including photocopying, recording, or by any information storage
and retrieval system, without permission in writing from the publisher.
Published by Clarkson N. Potter, Inc., 201 East 50th Street, New York, New York 10022, and
distributed by Crown Publishers, Inc. Member of the Crown Publishing Group
CLARKSON N. POTTER, POTTER, and colophon are trademarks of Clarkson N. Potter, Inc.
Manufactured in Japan
Library of Congress Cataloging-in-Publication Data
Conway, Patricia.
Art for everyday:the new craft movement/by Patricia Conway.
p.   cm.
1. Decorative arts—United States—History—20th century. 2. Design—United States—History—
20th century. I. Title.
NK808.C64   1990
745'.0973'0904—dc20   90-36609
CIP
ISBN 0-517-57381-4
10 9 8 7 6 5 4 3 2 1
First Edition

ACKNOWLEDGMENTS

Without the participation of a great many people, this book would not have been possible. Thanks to the collectors and admirers of contemporary craft, the artists working in the media, their gallery representatives, the museums dedicated to preserving the crafts ideal, and to many others who gave so generously of their time and resources, not only has this book been possible, it has been a pleasure to write.

I am especially grateful to those people, some of whom have chosen to remain anonymous, who permitted their homes and apartments to be photographed and their stories to be shared. For the first time, it is possible to show extensively how contemporary craft artists envision their work: not isolated in catalogs or exhibitions, but as part of everyday life. Understandably the artists were supportive of this effort, but many of them, like Rosanne Somerson and Alphonse Mattia, volunteered ideas and background information far beyond the scope of their individual careers. Similarly, the help provided by Warren and Bebe Johnson, owners of the Pritam & Eames Gallery, greatly exceeded professional interests. Not only did they make available furniture out of their gallery for photography at remote locations, but they gave much-needed technical advice, research assistance, and moral support. The Snyderman Gallery also lent furniture for photography, and two wonderful friends—Philip W. Pfeifer and Ted Nordman, proprietors of Le Cabinet Scientifique in Buckingham, Pennsylvania—provided locations. To the Johnsons, the Snydermans, and Le Cabinet Scientifique I wish to express special and very personal thanks.

Special thanks are due also to those people who so graciously shared their thoughts early-on in the development of this book: Jonathan Fairbanks, Director of the Boston Museum of Fine Arts; Edward S. Cooke, Assistant Curator of American Decorative Arts and Sculpture for the museum and organizer of the recent exhibition "New American Furniture"; Judy Coady, Assistant to the Director of the Renwick Gallery in Washington, D.C., and organizer of this country's first national collection of contemporary craft; and Marillyn Wilson, who, over nearly thirty years of observing the evolution of handmade furniture in America, has acquired a wealth of anecdotal and documentary information.

For help in documenting the early-twentieth-century craft movements, I am particularly indebted to Eduard F. Sekler, Professor of Architecture at Harvard University and author of the definitive work *Josef Hoffmann* (Princeton University Press, 1985). Professor Sekler's lectures on the Wiener Werkstätte were an inspiration, and his generosity in providing photographs of Hoffmann's interiors from his own archives is deeply appreciated. For the opportunity of studying with Professor Sekler and for the time to research the history of arts and crafts, I am also indebted to the Loeb Fellowship at the Harvard Graduate School of Design and, especially, to its sponsors, Mr. and Mrs. John L. Loeb.

Researching contemporary craft art was a formidable task, accomplished with boundless energy and unfailing good cheer by Dominique Lalli. Nica not only made hundreds of phone calls but was indispensable in arranging for photography and assisting Jon Jensen. Jon's photography brought this book to life. With an unerring eye for detail, a superb mastery of light, and without the dubious benefit of professional "styling," Jon managed to capture the spirit of both contemporary craft and those people who enjoy living with it. Elizabeth Van Itallie gave shape to this spirit. Her design skills and remarkable sensitivity to the subject matter imposed graphic order without ever compromising the essential freedom that distinguishes one-of-a-kind craft from commercial production. Nica, Jon, and Elizabeth were an excellent team, and I am grateful to Gael Towey, former Creative Director of Clarkson N. Potter, for bringing this team together and generating early concepts for producing this book.

The real heroine, as always, was my staff assistant, Marika Kurouklis, who documented this book. She, along with my editor, Carol Southern, maintained calm where chaos constantly threatened. Finally (but only in sequence of acknowledgment) there was my family. Once again they endured, and it is to them that I dedicate this book.

THE ARTS AND CRAFTS TRADITION 8

Turning the
  Century 10
Postwar Years 19

LIVING WITH CRAFT TODAY 25

Embassy Row 26
East Meets West (Coast) 32
Suburban Sophistication 40
Gallery Owners at
  Home 44
Can One Sit on a
  Clock? 53
On the Beach 56
From Town to Country 60
With Comfort in Mind 65
Manhattan Pied-à-terre 78
Weekends in the Village 86
A Family Tradition 91
The Art of Entertaining 94
Growing Up in SoHo 108
Brooklyn Neighbors 113
Woodland Retreat 118
Mission Accomplished 122
The Artist as Collector 127

THE ARCHITECTURAL CONNECTION 137

MONY Headquarters 138

CONT

The Rainbow Room 142
Christian Theological
    Seminary 146
Alaska Performing Arts
    Center 148
Home Box Office 150
Pandick Press Offices 154

THE ARTIST'S VISION   159

GLASS   160
Ray King 161
Susan Stinsmuehlen-
    Amend 166
Marni Bakst 168
Ellen Mandelbaum 172
Ed Carpenter 174

TILE   178
Constance Leslie 179
Elizabeth MacDonald 186
Betty Woodman 189

METAL   190
Albert Paley 191
Greg and Lydia Leavitt 197
Christopher Ray 200
Richard Johnston 202

FURNITURE   204
Rosanne Somerson 205
John Dunnigan 210
Wendy Maruyama 212
Alphonse Mattia 214
James Schriber 217
Thomas Hucker 218
Timothy Philbrick 221
Richard Scott Newman 223
Wendy Stayman 225
Bruce Volz 226
Michael Hurwitz 228
Peter Dean 230
Thomas Loeser 232
Judy Kensley McKie 234
Ronald Puckett 240
Gail Fredell Smith 242
Jack Larimore 244
Peter Spadone 246
Mitch Ryerson 248
Kristina Madsen 250
Garry Knox Bennett 252
Wendell Castle 254

Directory of Craft Galleries
    and Organizations 260

Index 262

THE ARTS AND CRAFTS TRADITION

At the turn of this century, craft in America was revered as "the art that is life"; by the late 1960s, it had become the art that was life-style. Along the way, it led a brave rebellion against the modern machine aesthetic; was proliferated as the stock-in-trade of thousands of little "shoppes"; declared high art by its backers; and pronounced dead by an architectural profession wary of both heresy and bad taste. Now, as the century draws to a close, an influential group of woodworkers, glass-makers, metalworkers, and ceramicists is renewing the ideal of craft as both a serious artistic pursuit and a part of everyday life.

*Massive built-in sideboard in the Kingscote
(Newport, Rhode Island) dining room, 1880.
OPPOSITE Robert Whitley's "Throne Chair,"
1978.*

TURNING THE CENTURY

Craft, according to *Webster's,* is simply "an occupation or trade requiring manual dexterity or artistic skill." But for the latter part of the nineteenth and the early twentieth centuries in both Great Britain and the United States, it was much more. Linked to a succession of social, economic, and aesthetic reform movements, craft was imbued with moral and philosophical qualities that eventually transcended the numerous styles with which it was associated. Many of our ideas about craft today can be traced to the late-nineteenth-century Arts and Crafts movement, even if some of the original socioeconomic theories underlying that movement have been discarded long since.

The origins of the Arts and Crafts movement in America, usually dated from 1875–1880 to 1916, are so intertwined with the Aesthetic movement (1875 to 1885) that were it not for one very basic difference, it would be impossible to distinguish the two. Both movements had antecedents in Great Britain about a decade earlier, both attempted to reform design, and both drew, stylistically, from Gothic and Oriental sources. Moreover, the Philadelphia Centennial Exposition of 1876 seems to have been an important catalyst for both, exhibiting decorative arts from around the world and, at the same time, reviving interest in American Colonial and craft-based design such as Shaker furniture. But in one important respect the two movements did differ. Whereas the emphasis in the Aesthetic movement was on surface decoration, Arts and Crafts design stressed form, function, structure, and the appropriateness of materials: "art for life's sake" versus "art for art's sake"; "plain living and high thinking" versus "sweetness and light"; the morality of craft versus the aesthetics of decoration. In many of its principles, the Arts and Crafts movement clearly anticipated the Modern movement, even though by 1920 the two had become polarized.

The legacy of Aestheticism is important to contemporary craft

The dining room added to Kingscote (Newport, Rhode Island) by Stanford White in 1880–1881 is considered to be the finest interior of the Aesthetic period. In its simplicity, abstract lines, predominant use of wood, and integration of furniture with architecture, it anticipates both the Arts and Crafts movement and Modern design. Opalescent glass bricks around fireplace are by Louis Comfort Tiffany, Associated Artists.

The dining room of the J. B. E. Corbin house in Nancy, France, also displays a predominance of wood and integration of furniture with architecture, but in the flamboyant curvilinear style of Art Nouveau, another offshoot of the Aesthetic movement. Furnishings were designed and made by French woodworker Eugène Vallin, 1903–1906.

not only because it was out of this movement that Arts and Crafts evolved but because the collaborative nature of Aestheticism is the most recent and most convincing model for the reconnection of craft and architecture. Indeed, the Aesthetic movement provided an opportunity for collaboration so unprecedented that many major artists expanded their roles across previously established boundaries and some even joined forces in the rapidly growing business of professional decorating.

In 1879, the painter Louis Comfort Tiffany (with landscape artist Samuel Colman, textile and wallpaper designer Candace Wheeler, and ornamental woodworker Lockwood DeForest) founded Associated Artists—one of the most prominent of the decorating firms. Their inspiration was the decorating work of American painter James Abbott McNeill Whistler, whose Peacock Room for the home of a British industrialist was—and still is—one of the most famous interiors in the world. Whistler's work proved that painters no longer had to confine their art to the easel, that they could embellish walls, decorate furniture, or ornament tiles. Similarly, architects were encouraged to go beyond building plans and exterior elevations, to design interiors, furniture, metalwork, tilework, and other decorative elements of which the ornamentation of Frank Furness and Louis Sullivan is perhaps the best-known example.

This harmonious interplay of art, craft, and architecture is less evident in the Arts and Crafts movement not only because the latter retreated from high art (*usefulness* was the watchword of early Arts and Crafts writers) but because there was in the Arts and Crafts movement a communal tendency that, in practice, sometimes valued social goals over artistic competence. In other words, where Aestheticism was characterized by an intense professionalism, Arts and Crafts was obliged, for philosophical reasons, to absorb a certain amount of amateurism or hobbyism.

A good example is the Roycrofters Community founded in 1894 by Elbert Hubbard in East Aurora, New York. Initially dedicated to bookmaking and associated arts, the Roycrofters rapidly expanded into the production of furniture, ornamental ironwork, and china. They built their own shops and houses, provided for their own education, established an apprenticeship system, organized lectures, and, by 1900, were operating their own Roycroft Inn for visitors to the community. However, their ideal of the unity of all

TOP Dining room of Josef Hoffmann's Stoclet house, Brussels, 1905–1911. Walls are Paonazzo marble, and the buffets Portovenere marble with Macassar wood; mosaic panels are by Gustav Klimt. ABOVE Great hall of Hoffmann's Skywa-Primavesi house, Vienna-Hietzing, 1913. Paneling is carved and polished oak; lighting and floor covering are later additions.

crafts soon led to well-intentioned dilettantism: one person with no particular talent participating in half a dozen different crafts. The result, as observed by Janet Ashbee, the wife of pioneering British Arts and Crafts architect Charles Robert Ashbee, was an absence of any real artistic sensibility within the community. Writing from America, she described how Roycrofters "in the intervals of bookmaking lend a hand to spread mortar or adjust a corner stone." Such interchangeability of skills, she felt, produced "queer stuff . . . all colors and types and papers and bindings with now and then a successful fluke."

Another reason for the lesser role of collaboration in Arts and Crafts was the ascendance of architects as the master builders, the ultimate form givers of the movement. Although there is much about American Arts and Crafts that was unique to this country, basically the Americans looked to Great Britain and, to a lesser extent, the Continent for their ideas; and in Great Britain and on the Continent, the Arts and Crafts movement was dominated by architects and architectural theory. The leaders of the English movement, which had its origins in the earlier nineteenth-century criticism of reformers A. W. N. Pugin and John Ruskin, were mostly trained in architecture before they branched out into interior design, furniture, and the decorative arts: C. R. Ashbee, C. F. A. Voysey, A. H. Mackmurdo, Philip Webb, W. R. Lethaby, M. H. Baillie Scott. Even the protean William Morris studied architecture briefly before taking up pattern design and, in 1861, founding the decorating firm of Morris, Marshall, Faulkner & Co., through which he became the single most influential figure in Arts

Entrance hall of Charles Rennie Mackintosh's Hill House, Helensburgh, Scotland, 1903–1904. Space is unified through repetition of squares in woodwork, furniture, rugs, and lighting fixtures.

ABOVE Interior view of a Gustav Stickley house, ca. 1910. RIGHT July 1903 issue of The Craftsman *featured this rendering of dining room by Harvey Ellis, the most talented of the architects employed by Stickley. Elements of Ellis's designs recall the work of British Arts and Crafts architects C. R. Mackintosh and M. H. Baillie Scott. BELOW Living room of Charles Sumner Greene and Henry Mather Greene's Gamble house, Pasadena, California, 1908–1909. The reliance on materials and construction, emphasis on horizontal planes, and inglenook with built-in furniture are typical of American Arts and Crafts architecture. Piano and carpet design are also by Greene and Greene.*

and Crafts on both sides of the Atlantic. When the British came to America (to lecture, to tour the Arts and Crafts communities, to visit the settlement houses), they invariably came away being most impressed with Charles Sumner Greene, Henry Mather Greene, and Frank Lloyd Wright—architects whose work is the crowning achievement of the American Arts and Crafts movement. Both the Greene brothers and Wright were known for designing their own furniture, architectural glass, metalwork, and other decorative elements, using craft as their idiom and craft methods for the production of their work, but not usually acknowledging direct participation of other artists or craftspeople in the design process. The result is an aesthetic unity not unlike that found in the rigorously controlled interiors of Glasgow architect Charles Rennie Mackintosh and the Viennese architects Josef Hoffmann and Adolf Loos.

Of the three, Loos—a puritanical reformer who equated ornament with crime—came closest in his design to the characteristic severity of American Arts and Crafts architecture, while Mackintosh and Hoffmann were more influenced by the other turn-of-the-century movement that evolved out of Aestheticism, namely Art Nouveau. In many ways a Continental reworking of the ideas of William Morris, Art Nouveau emerged in Brussels and Paris in the 1890s, by which time the American Arts and Crafts movement had already assimilated most of its influences from Great Britain. For this reason, there are only minimal traces of Art Nouveau in American Arts and Crafts, notably in the graphic arts,

BELOW LEFT Dining room of Frank Lloyd Wright's Meyer May house, Grand Rapids, Michigan, 1909. Although noted for designing all furniture, architectural glass, metalwork, and other decorative elements for his houses, Wright did, in fact, have collaborators. Chief among them was Milwaukee interior designer George Mann Neidecken, who painted the hollyhock mural BELOW RIGHT on wall separating dining room from entry hall. Note that lights on corner piers of table repeat design of copper-camed clear and colored glass windows wrapping room.

the work of Louis Comfort Tiffany, and in architectural ornamentation such as that of Louis Sullivan. In the designs of Mackintosh and Hoffmann, the sinuous curves of Art Nouveau were tamed, the floral motifs abstracted, and asymmetry gave way to a fairly strict rectilinearity. Yet, despite certain stylistic similarities, the attitudes of these two architects toward the Arts and Crafts tradition in which they both worked were quite different. Mackintosh, whose early work was more highly acclaimed in Vienna than in Scotland, had little use for craftsmanship per se: He was not much interested in how his furniture and interior decorations got built, only in designing them to be part of a unified, organic whole. Hoffmann, while equally insistent upon coherent, carefully coordinated interiors, was able to achieve the unity he wanted by collaborating with numerous artists and craftspeople to whom he gave complete artistic freedom.

Despite the generally Progressive and, at times, socialist politics that went along with Arts and Crafts, the fact is that most of what the leading architects in the movement produced could be afforded only by the wealthy. It fell to two nonarchitects to democratize the legacy of Ruskin and Morris, to popularize the Arts and Crafts ideal for the broad middle class. These two people were Elbert Hubbard, the retired soapmaker/mass marketer/advertiser who founded the Roycroft Community, and Gustav Stickley, the commercial furniture maker turned craftsman and polemicist who, in 1898, formed the Gustav Stickley Company in Eastwood, near Syracuse, New York. In April 1901, Stickley began publication of *The Craftsman,* a widely read magazine that promoted everything from the work of William Morris, Greene and Greene, and Louis Sullivan to Stickley's own Mission-style furniture. In addition, *The Craftsman* each month published plans and drawings of inexpensive bungalows, or "Craftsman Homes" as Stickley called them.

With the December 1916 issue, *The Craftsman* ceased publication. Financially overextended, Stickley had filed for bankruptcy the year before. World War I was sweeping away the old order everywhere, and with it, the Arts and Crafts movement.

Living room of Wright's Meyer May house OPPOSITE and RIGHT illustrates the total integration of architecture, furniture, fixtures, and decorative detailing that was the ideal of much Arts and Crafts design. Patterning of art-glass windows is picked up in embroidered table runners, woven into carpets, and repeated at larger scale in oak moldings applied to ceilings, walls, and window frames. BELOW Dresser and bedstead for the house of Mrs. Lawrence Demmer, Milwaukee, ca. 1904. The construction is commercial millwork, probably by F. H. Bresler Company, and the design is by George Mann Niedecken, the interior designer who also collaborated with Wright in furnishing the May house.

Refurbished dining room of the Eliel Saarinen house at Cranbrook, although somewhat simplified from the original, is still extraordinary for its meticulous detailing and integration of custom-designed furniture with architecture. Designed 1928–1930, the table and chairs are Art Deco in style.

POSTWAR YEARS

▼

The principal links between the Arts and Crafts movement that ended in 1916 and the revival of handcraft following World War II were the Bauhaus, founded in Weimar in 1919, and the Cranbrook Academy of Art, founded 1927–1932 in Bloomfield Hills, Michigan, with Finnish architect Eliel Saarinen as its first president. Combining a restrained Classicism with the Arts and Crafts legacy of his work in Finland and Europe between 1890 and 1910, Saarinen designed buildings, interiors, furniture, and fixtures for the new campus in a richly detailed manner that came to be known as the Cranbrook style. Unlike the Bauhaus, where the early goal of unifying all the arts through craft soon gave way to a machine-based aesthetic, the Cranbrook Academy never lost touch with its Arts and Crafts origins.

Ironically, however, it was the Bauhaus, and not Cranbrook, that stimulated the postwar revival of handcraft. Reacting against the coldness of tubular steel and glass—the hallmarks of Bauhaus-inspired furniture, which, by the 1950s and 1960s, defined the leading edge of industrial design in America—a sculptor named Wharton Esherick, then in his sixties, began to attract an audience for the somewhat eccentric furniture he designed and produced in his Paoli, Pennsylvania, studio. A brilliant craftsman, Esherick inspired many younger artists to explore the nature of wood and give it an organic form that expressed its inherent qualities. Other mostly self-taught woodworkers such as George Nakashima, Sam Maloof, Arthur Espenet Carpenter, and, in England, John Makepeace, pursued this direction throughout the 1950s and 1960s, forming the nucleus

In the same year that Saarinen completed his dining room, sculptor Wharton Esherick installed this spiral staircase in his Paoli, Pennsylvania, studio. Rough-hewn red oak steps project from twisted Y-shaped trunk "like the stubs of pruned branches." In its tree-form conception, the stair can be seen today as a prototype for organic woodworking that emerged in the craft revival following World War II.

19

of what was to become known as the first generation of postwar craftsmen, some of whom, although now in their later years, are still active.

But it was the Danish furniture maker Tage Frid who, more than any other woodworker, coalesced the craft revival. Recruited by the School for American Craftsmen (SAC, founded in 1944 at Dartmouth College and relocated to Alfred University in 1946), Frid arrived in 1948 to teach what was then the only college-level program in this country offering a major in furniture making. When, in 1950, the SAC program moved to the Rochester Institute of Technology (RIT) and again, in 1962, to the Rhode Island School of Design (RISD), Frid moved with it, establishing a strong technical foundation for a discipline characterized early on by more interest in the "freedom" of material than in technique. Two of Frid's most distinguished students became major influences in their own right: Jere Osgood, a powerful designer; and Dan Jackson, an inspired teacher who headed the furniture program at the Philadelphia College of Art (PCA) at its founding in 1964 and, with Osgood, helped to set up the Program in Artisanry (PIA) at Boston University in 1975. Along with James Krenov—an American-born, Swedish-trained woodworker as well known for his writing and criticism as for his furniture—Frid, Osgood, and Jackson are regarded as seminal figures for the second generation that began to emerge in the mid-1970s.

Although many of these second-generation furniture makers have been taught by the first generation, their work departs radically from that of their mentors, both visually and conceptually. Whereas the first generation had come out of the apprentice system and created mostly functional furniture in a naturalistic, ahistorical manner or hybrid Shaker–Scandinavian style that emphasized the spirituality and primacy of wood, the second generation are mostly school-trained artists who draw on historical style, traditional furniture making, architecture, industrial design, folk art, and mixed media to create highly sophisticated pieces that sometimes border on sculpture. To distinguish this second generation from the first, critics often describe their output as "art furniture" rather than "woodworking."

The career that best illustrates this transition is that of woodworker/sculptor Wendell

OPPOSITE *James Krenov's spalted maple music stand, 1987, and his pearwood "Walkaround" cabinet, 1986. LEFT Fiddleback maple rocking chair first designed by Sam Maloof ca. 1960 is still available on commission. Bubinga and ash writing desk BELOW LEFT is by Jere Osgood, 1985. Three of six laminated and scrubbed oak "Espalier" dining chairs BELOW made by John Makepeace in 1983 at his School for Craftsmen in Wood, Dorset, England. The chairs and a table were commissioned for a private residence that looks out at a woodland.*

Castle (pages 254 to 259), who began in the 1960s making organic wood furniture out of stack-laminated and carved masses that departed completely from the stick-and-board tradition that other first-generation woodworkers had continued to respect. Critics saw Castle's work as the ultimate rejection of machine-made furniture, which, although produced in industrial materials, was still based on stick-and-board construction. Then, in 1967, Castle produced a molded plastic chair in the same carved-mass form as his stack-laminated pieces, proving that this modern industrial material, which had taken on negative connotations in the 1950s, could be used with originality and integrity. In the mid-1970s, Castle again departed from the first-generation woodworkers with whom he was initially associated: Taking up stick-and-board construction, he embellished it with trompe l'oeil flourishes, inlaid it with precious metals, and, in short, pushed furniture making as far away from naturalism and organic form as it could go.

Paralleling the second-generation attitude toward furniture making, there also occurred in glassmaking, metalworking, and ceramics a renewed interest in architectural application. For most of the first thirty years following World War II, these crafts had been abandoned by modern architects working in the unadorned Interna-

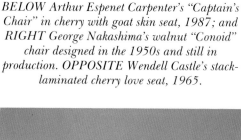

BELOW Arthur Espenet Carpenter's "Captain's Chair" in cherry with goat skin seat, 1987; and RIGHT George Nakashima's walnut "Conoid" chair designed in the 1950s and still in production. OPPOSITE Wendell Castle's stack-laminated cherry love seat, 1965.

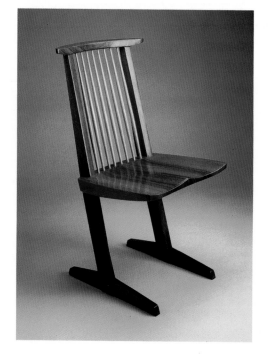

tional or Bauhaus style. Consequently, production had shifted to smaller-scale art pieces: precious objects enshrined under glass by institutions such as the American Craft Museum, founded in 1956. But with the advent of Post Modernism came a freer attitude toward ornament in architecture, an attitude that once again admitted to the possibility of collaboration with art and craft. No longer relegated to reproducing traditional designs for churches or historic restorations, the architectural crafts re-emerged with youthful vigor and an insatiable appetite for innovation.

It is the work of these second-generation furniture makers, these glassmakers, metalworkers, and ceramicists that is documented in this book. With backgrounds in everything from the fine arts, architecture, and industrial design to psychology and even theology, these mostly young craft artists (their average age is somewhere in the early forties) work in a dazzling array of styles that look nothing like the Arts and Crafts aesthetic of the early part of this century. Yet, in one respect, these contemporary artists are the direct descendants of that movement: They believe in the unifying moral and artistic force of craft and in the reconnection of that force with architecture. They are designing not for museums and collectors only, but for people's homes, their work places, their public buildings. They are shaping space, illuminating it, and filling our lives with functional objects that are the art of everyday.

Chairs by Jack Larimore and table by Bob Trotman frame view from the northern California home of Andy and Ginny Lewis. Dining room OPPOSITE is furnished with table and chairs by woodworker Robert Whitley.

LIVING WITH CRAFT TODAY

Craft is seductive. It is beautiful to look at and inviting to touch. It is important enough, artistically, to be displayed in museums, but it can be sat upon, eaten at, and slept on, too. China can be stored in it, hats hung on it, term papers written at it. Collectors may catalogue it along with their Picassos and Matisses, but most people just stuff letters in it and curl up on it with a good book. In fact, one of the nicest things about living with craft is that behind each piece there is a story —the story of the artist who made it, the moment in which it was commissioned, the events surrounding its completion. Prowling galleries in search of new artists can be as thrilling as big-game hunting. As more people are discovering that thrill, their homes and apartments testify to the pleasures of craft as a part of everyday life.

EMBASSY ROW

Careful placement of Bruce Volz's statuary pedestals in the sparsely furnished entry hall RIGHT gives added dignity to both the space and the pieces. Pedestals are handmade paper, marble, and gold leaf over wood, 1987. Hall table BELOW is by Steven Whitney; bubinga, ebony, and holly, 1987.

Contemporary furniture artists, lacking the unifying aesthetic of the historical crafts movements, work in a sometimes bewildering array of styles that can challenge even the most knowledgeable collector wishing to create visually harmonious surroundings. The solution is either to limit purchases to work that is stylistically compatible, or to hire a designer who can pull it all together.

David Schwarz of David M. Schwarz Architectural Services, Washington, D.C., had two such challenging commissions to his credit—the Abramson apartment (pages 94 to 107) and the Joseph apartment (pages 64 to 77)—when he undertook the gut renovation of this 1923 house just off Washington's Embassy Row. The client, a bachelor, owned an impressive collection of 1920s and 1930s art glass, contemporary ceramics, building images from 1900 to 1960, Art Deco furniture, and contemporary art/craft pieces that had to be accommodated without compromising the new owner's principal intention for the house: "living there with slews of guests."

Completed in 1988–1989, the redesigned house not only absorbs this mix

In the living room OPPOSITE Bruce Volz's
"American Flyer II" cabinet (open, RIGHT) is
perfectly located between arched windows,
providing a contemporary counterpoint for the
grouping of Art Deco lounge chairs from the Ile
de France around coffee table by Art Deco
designer Jacques-Emile Ruhlmann. Cabinet is
holly, ebonized cherry, brass, silk, and ceramic
beads, 1986. Table is rosewood, silvered bronze,
and ivory, ca. 1930. Chairs with silvered bronze
feet are upholstered in moiré fabric.
ABOVE Wendell Castle's "Sub-Nine" coffee
table; East India ebony and dark blue leather,
1988. FAR RIGHT Castle's cabinet entitled
"He Came Without His Wallet"; stained curly
maple veneer, solid maple, bronze, Colorcore,
and rubber, 1986. ABOVE RIGHT Bed by
James Schriber; curly maple, 1986.

without a trace of clutter, contradiction, or self-consciousness but adds new meaning to the work of artists whose impulses are as disparate as Wendell Castle and James Schriber. Seldom is so much contemporary craft furniture seen in an environment that makes it appear so "right," so inevitable. Yet the owner, who prefers purchasing to commissioning, did not buy pieces specifically for the house, nor did Schwarz design the interior for specific pieces. "I buy what I like," explains the owner, "and the things that I like are what is, or was, on the cutting edge at the time of its design." Much of his contemporary art/craft furniture was bought "with the idea of eventually moving to the country and mixing it with American Arts and Crafts furniture—Stickley, for example"—which makes the elegance imparted to these pieces by Schwarz's design all the more remarkable.

For Schwarz himself, a sympathetic response to art/craft furnishings is second nature. "We [the firm] tend to use craft furniture whenever we're doing interiors, not because all of our clients are collectors but because, when they say 'give us furniture,' that's what we recommend." A collector in his own right, Schwarz grew up with the contemporary craft movement. "My father ran a woodworking store," he recalls, "and he was a friend of Sam Maloof. I think anybody who claims to be interested in design and doesn't know what furniture artists are doing today is just not well informed." Clearly, this client is informed, and Schwarz's design reveals the architect's deep respect for that information.

*Library features two game tables by Ron Puckett
DETAIL ABOVE with "Costes" chairs by
contemporary French designer Philipe Starke.
Tables are bubinga and wenge, 1988.*

EAST MEETS WEST (COAST)

Had Paul and Gloria Choi not elected to do part of their professional training in Rochester, New York, where woodworker Wendell Castle has his studio, the Choi home might not be the remarkable place that it is today. As it happened, a gallery across from Paul's office was displaying a piece of Castle's furniture the evening Gloria was waiting outside for her husband, who was working late. Intrigued by the piece, Gloria investigated and ultimately commissioned Castle to make a living room coffee table with a wood base and glass top—a combination that Castle had not previously explored. The result was so pleasing to the Chois that they went on to complete the furnishing of their small apartment with Castle's work.

That was 1977 and the beginning of an enduring personal relationship with Castle based on true collaboration between patron and artist. The Chois have since settled in the Bay Area of San Francisco and, at last count, have amassed some twenty-six pieces of art/craft furniture. Collectors by nature (their walls are hung with lithographs and prints by Miro, Arp, Delaunay, and Goetz), the Chois continue to buy and

Paul and Gloria Choi and their daughter, Dezraye, enjoy the formality imparted by objectlike pieces such as Wendell Castle's 1977 dining table ABOVE. Carved and laminated in walnut, it is designed with a lazy Susan that removes to reveal sensuous open swirl DETAIL OPPOSITE. The chairs were made four years later, during period when Castle was exploring marquetry and other fine furniture techniques. Marquetry inlays, made by woodworker Silas Kopf, depict the four seasons, the sun, and the moon.

commission special pieces, rotating them in and out of a basement storage area so that they can enjoy an exciting but uncluttered domestic landscape.

That landscape is formal yet functional: The art of furniture is central to the Chois' acquisitions, but no more so than comfort and utility. Their ten-year-old daughter, Dezraye, who once spooned pabulum from a high chair made for her by Castle, now does her homework at a Garry Knox Bennett desk; her backyard playhouse is furnished with Castle's "Molar" chairs and table. "Some of my friends think our furniture is weird," admits Dezraye, but Wendy Maruyama's "Mickey Mackintosh" chair (one of a series, page 132) is her proudest possession. Recently, she received a dollhouse from woodworker Norman Petersen, and Maruyama is making a miniature chair for it.

The Choi home is a study in controlled

Living room of the Choi home LEFT is dominated by Wendell Castle's carved and laminated rosewood coffee table with glass top, 1977, and his carved and laminated walnut wall-hung sideboard, 1979, shown open ABOVE. The polychromed wood chairs upholstered with suede-covered rolls are by Norman Petersen, 1986.

BELOW *Gail Fredell Smith's stained and painted buffet, 1982, shown here with one of Castle's dining chairs; and Garry Knox Bennett's painted wood, Colorcore, and aluminum desk with gold- and silver-plated metal clock and lamp, 1986. Paired with desk is Norman Petersen's chair in lacquered wood with gold and silver paint, and polychromed leather upholstery by K. Lee Manuel.*
Details of one of Petersen's living room chairs LEFT, *Smith's buffet* RIGHT, *and Bennett's desk* FAR RIGHT *reveal the Choi's interest in bold color and strong design. Patterning on front of desk is achieved by laminating Colorcore, then milling, slicing, and reassembling it.*

Daughter Dezraye reads outside her garden playhouse, furnished with Wendell Castle's molded plastic "Molar" chairs, 1967. Her walnut high chair FAR RIGHT was made for her by Castle in 1979. Castle's two-seat bench, another excellent example of the period when he was exploring organic form, is carved and laminated cherry, 1977. RIGHT.

eclecticism: Chinese heirloom pieces take their places next to contemporary art/craft furnishings; antique Chinese vases mix with modern ceramics and glasswork; elaborate detail is offset by stark white walls. Having begun their art/craft furniture collection on the East Coast shortly after arriving in this country from Malaysia, the Chois now buy and commission almost exclusively West Coast artists such as Gail Fredell Smith, Norman Petersen, Bennett, and Maruyama. In each case, they have left full design control in the hands of the artist. An example is the credenza by Wendy Maruyama (see page 213): Paul told her only what kind of piece he wanted and did not even ask to see it until it was finished. "Wendy was very nervous," recalls Paul, "but we like being surprised."

SUBURBAN SOPHISTICATION

"We're not really collectors," says Barbara Fendrick, who, with her husband, Daniel, owns The Fendrick Gallery in Georgetown (Washington, D.C.) and the Barbara Fendrick Gallery in SoHo (New York City). "We buy art because we love it, because we can't live without it, and because, as dealers, we have a responsibility to support our artists even if it means eating hamburgers." The gracious mix of antiques, family heirlooms, fine paintings, prints, sculpture, and art/craft furniture in the house where they've raised five children attests to this philosophy. Barbara Fendrick, who represents both Wendell Castle and Albert Paley, regards these artists' work as primarily sculpture. Yet the pieces she has chosen for her own home fit so easily into the environment that their function as furniture is unquestionable.

"To be interesting, a house has to be eclectic, it has to span time," Fendrick believes. "Just having paintings is not enough. It is objects that give dimension to space." Ironically, Fendrick's first Castle purchase—an oversized pair of Pop Art eyeglasses that he had carved in cherry before she began to represent him—is an object that has still not found a place in her home. "I've watched Wendell's evolution

The Fendricks' 1920s house LEFT opens onto vegetable garden seen here beyond Albert Paley's forged and fabricated mild steel plant stand, 1981. RIGHT Detail of Paley's glass-topped dining table; forged and fabricated mild steel with brass, 1981.

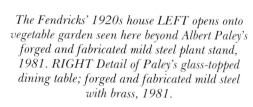

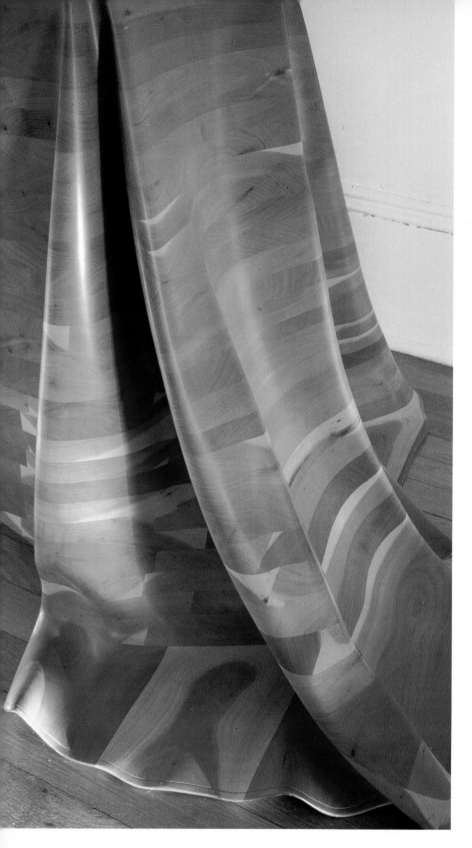

from stack lamination and trompe l'oeil. Wendell's genius is staying ahead of the people he teaches. He's the Jacques-Emile Ruhlmann [the Art Deco furniture designer] of the present day."

Since they bought their house twenty years ago, the Fendricks have achieved their notion of eclecticism with great sophistication: Canvases by Helen Frankenthaler, William Bailey, Jasper Johns, Robert Motherwell, and other noted artists offset Castle's and Paley's furniture. They still buy occasionally, but the fact that nothing in their home is for sale has slowed down the Fendricks' rate of acquisition considerably. "We maintain a strict separation between our galleries and our home. And right now, our home is just about filled up."

ABOVE AND LEFT Wendell Castle's laminated and carved cherry trompe l'oeil "Cloth Without Table," 1979, plays a dual role, mediating between art and warm, comfortable furnishings. RIGHT The library, with another glass-topped Albert Paley table in forged and fabricated mild steel with brass, 1981. The wire, mud, and straw horse sculpture is by Deborah Butterfield, and the vase in the window is a self-portrait entitled "Funny Vace" by Robert Arneson, a ceramicist turned sculptor.

GALLERY OWNERS AT HOME

Since they opened the Pritam & Eames Gallery in East Hampton, New York, in 1981, Warren and Bebe Johnson (he was formerly a filmmaker, she was trained as an anthropologist) have been among the leading art/craft furniture dealers in the country. Therefore, it is not surprising that their own home is filled with pieces acquired over the years from some of the artists they represent. What is surprising, however, is the unassuming ease with which the Johnsons have adapted furniture that is their business to the everyday routines of their private lives.

Unlike many art dealers, Warren and Bebe do not treat their home as an extension of their gallery. There are no de rigueur white walls, no "drop dead" decorator touches. The interior walnut trim typical of the era (ca. 1910) has been restored

The Johnsons' front door, of painted clear pine, was made by Long Island woodworker David Ebner in 1985. At left of door is Timothy Philbrick's tea table in kosipo and slate with palm nut feet, 1986. Above the table is Richard Scott Newman's mahogany- and ebony-framed mirror, 1988. Table to right of door DETAIL OPPOSITE was made by Ted Hawke in maple with inlays of various woods, 1986.

FAR LEFT TOP are John Dunnigan's chair (bubinga, upholstered in Ultrasuede, 1987) and stool (cherry, 1988); and BOTTOM George Gordon's mahogany rocker with Jack Lenor Larsen's woven leather upholstery, 1987. IMMEDIATE LEFT is Johnson dining room display cabinet made by Ron Puckett in padouk, ebonized mahogany, and beaten copper, 1984. Another view of Johnson dining room RIGHT shows James Krenov's mahogany and yucca cabinet, 1988; and Hank Gilpin's cherry chair with Jack Lenor Larsen fabric, 1987. BELOW Warren, Bebe, and Rani Johnson in front of their eastern Long Island home.

to its natural finish (by Warren himself, who has done all of the renovation work on the house); the coziness of relatively small rooms is enhanced with a deep green paint finish beneath the dark chair-rail molding. Furnishings are placed not so much with an eye to their "importance" as with deference to the practical constraints of room size and family life—which is very down-to-earth.

Nor do the Johnsons "churn" their collection by retiring older acquisitions when new ones arrive. Instead, they gradually have been replacing mass-produced or antique furnishings with pieces that they "have simply fallen in love with and plan to keep forever." At the moment, the mix of old favorites, recent acquisitions, commissions, antiques, and plain ordinary furniture is so skillful that, at first glance, it is

very hard to tell which pieces are which.

A good example is the dining room: The table was in the house when the Johnsons bought it (they've since commissioned James Schriber to replace it with "something special"); the chairs are from a limited edition by Hank Gilpin, with upholstery fabric by Jack Lenor Larsen; the display cabinet is a recent work by James Krenov; the chandelier is "a piece we

OPPOSITE *Rosanne Somerson's reading couch and Judy Kensley McKie's "Snake" table keep company in Johnson sun room. Reading couch is bleached wenge, 1987; "Snake" table is carved and painted maple, 1988. On wall behind Somerson's couch is her mirror of wenge, paint, and handmade paper, 1986. Lamp is by Joseph Tracy; paper and silk, 1988.*

The Johnsons serve picnics and summer cocktails from Bennett Bean's terra-cotta, slate, and steel table 1987, OPPOSITE. Bruce Beeken's cedar chair, 1982, has survived eight seasons out of doors.

found in a secondhand fixture shop years ago"; the rug is a gift from a friend of Bebe's; and the china cabinet was made by Ron Puckett in 1984.

Each of the Johnsons' pieces is in daily use and none is off limits to their daughter, Rani—nor, for that matter, to Max, the family's Labrador retriever, or to the two cats. "We wouldn't dream of having something we couldn't sit down on, serve drinks

from, or eat off of," says Bebe, and their Adirondack-style chair by Bruce Beeken is proof of her earnestness; it has sat, unprotected, in the Johnsons' backyard every summer since 1983. "We believe strongly in the aesthetic and the art of contemporary craft furniture," emphasizes Warren; "that's why we're devoting our careers to it. But the real test of any piece is how comfortably one can live with it."

CAN ONE SIT ON A CLOCK?

For Alexander "Sandy" Milliken, dealing in art and living with the work of artists whose medium is furniture are interchangeable experiences. "Bettina [his wife] and I were accumulating pieces at home until I realized that, in order to go on collecting, I had to become a dealer. Now I wonder what will happen when one of our children is asked to make a picture of a desk and draws a piece of furniture that has twenty legs."

The piece to which he refers is Wendell Castle's "Temple Desk," which, with its matching chair, has long been a focal point of the loft in which the Milliken children are growing up. Although, like all of his Wendell Castle and Albert Paley pieces, the desk and chair are for sale through his namesake gallery, Milliken is ambivalent about the possibility of having to part with them. "I once took that desk and chair out of the living room and it felt so empty. But if I want to stay in touch with

Milliken bedroom RIGHT with Wendell Castle's trompe l'oeil chest of drawers carved in Honduras mahogany, 1980. OPPOSITE Detail of Castle's trompe l'oeil "Table with Gloves and Keys," carved in purpleheart, 1981.

new work, I have to sell. I can't stand the thought of putting things like this in storage where no one will ever see them."

Milliken views the work of Castle and Paley as livable sculpture. "I never think about craft, except that I do believe every artist should have one. Everything should be beautifully made. But it's the intensity, the vision, the strength of these artists' work that make me want to have it in my home. And these pieces function, too. That's what's so remarkable about them."

What is also remarkable about Castle's work, according to Milliken, is the way Castle uses a broad range of historical knowledge and traditional skills to make people look at familiar things in new ways. A good example is the series of thirteen

clocks made by Castle in 1984–1985, each one of which is accompanied by a narrative. The "Magician's Birthday" clock that stands in the Milliken living room is Castle's conception of time in the medieval period, when clocks were considered magical. Its form personifies a cone-hatted magician, with the magician's trick rings at its peak. It stands on twelve feet, representing the twelve hours in a day and the twelve inches in a foot. Each foot is encircled with a gold-plated brass ring and a number that the magician has transposed from the face of the clock. "Castle claims that if one says the magic word, the numbers will jump back up on the face," explains Milliken, "but he's never told me what the magic word is."

ABOVE LEFT Castle's "Table with Gloves and Keys" and "Magician's Birthday" clock. One of thirteen tall-case clocks that Castle made in 1984–1985, this one, like the other twelve, has obvious anthropomorphic references and a text that explains its interpretation of time. It is fitted with a wind movement and executed in ebonized cherry, East Indian ebony, Gaboon ebony, and gold-plated brass. The "Temple Desk and Chair" ABOVE RIGHT, made in 1984, incorporate forms also used in the "Magician's Birthday" clock. The desk is ebonized imbuya, Osage orange, and ebony with 23K gold plating. The chair is ebonized imbuya with 23K gold plating and Persian lamb upholstery. Castle made the Australian lacewood paneling for the Milliken library ABOVE CENTER in 1984. Table is by Albert Paley; forged mild steel and glass, 1982.

Another of the thirteen Castle clocks, "Four Years Before Lunch: Grandson in Hawaiian Shirt"; satinwood, Swiss pearwood, Gaboon ebony, and bubinga, with a ten-line poem about time by Edward Lucie-Smith engraved on the back, 1984. Amidst toys is one of Castle's early molded plastic "Molar" chairs, 1967.

ON THE BEACH

The clear bright light picks out details of a John Dunnigan table and two Judy McKie chairs in a way that makes these pieces seem to fill the two-story dining room of Sheila and Eugene Heller's beach house. This is the family's second home, and the art/craft furnishings so carefully chosen for it are a perfect foil for the minimalist interior that frames ocean views beyond.

During the summer, Sheila, a psychotherapist, transports her notes to the beach house, where Ben Mack's gently curving desk (except for a standard wooden chair, the only piece of furniture in her second-floor study) provides an appropriately reflective work environment. Downstairs, McKie's "Dog Eat Dog" coffee table, a whimsical painted wood sculpture surmounted by a glass top, centers the living room. The intensity of the Dunnigan, Mack, and McKie pieces—the nucleus of the Hellers' growing collection—is greatly magnified by the coolness of their setting.

The Hellers bought their first art/craft furniture in 1982 and, as Sheila puts it, they've "been hooked ever since." Their motives for acquiring new pieces are simple: "We buy something because we love

it or because we need it" (e.g., the Dunnigan dining table). Sometimes they admire a piece so much that they create a space especially for it, as in the case of a Jere Osgood desk that now has pride of place in their year-round house. "We looked at that desk for two years, thinking, someday we'll find room for it. Then we bought it and renovated to *make* room for it."

Sheila and her husband collect together, recently involving their older son, Bruce, who has begun to show an interest in art/craft furniture. The rest of the household—two other children and a dog—take it all for granted. "We *live* with our collection," says Sheila, "we don't display it." Nor do the Hellers "buy names," although it is the work of known artists that often attracts them to gallery shows, where they discover appealing pieces by newer, less well-established people. Like many collectors, the Hellers buy through one gallery, with which they have a close personal relationship. "The gallery, like the furniture, is an important part of our lives."

During summer months, Sheila Heller retires to her second-floor ocean-view study to work at Ben Mack's curly maple desk, 1985.

The Hellers' beach house dining area RIGHT is furnished with John Dunnigan's oak and wenge table, 1984; and Judy Kensley McKie's "Jungle" chairs, also made in 1984, DETAIL OPPOSITE. Chairs are butternut, polychromed and carved with animal figures. BELOW Detail of McKie's glass-topped "Dog Eat Dog" table, a highly animated piece that shows to great advantage in the Hellers' minimalist living room. Table is polychromed wood, 1986.

FROM TOWN TO COUNTRY

Formerly codirector of The Gallery at Workbench and, with her husband, Pat, a pioneering sponsor of the contemporary craft-furniture movement, Judy Coady relaxes in James Schriber's oak garden chair made in 1984. Judy is now assistant to the director of the Renwick Gallery in Washington, D.C., and Pat is U.S. executive director of the World Bank. OPPOSITE One of the Coadys' more recent acquisitions, a console by the seminal woodworker Wharton Esherick. The table, made by Esherick in 1932, is padouk and bent oak. Visible beyond the table is one of the chairs Esherick made out of ax handles for a low-budget summer theater project.

It was the 1969 show "Objects USA" that transformed Judy Coady and her husband, Pat, from admirers of small crafts, mostly ceramics, into members of what the *New York Times* many years later described as "a new breed [of collectors] . . . one part connoisseur, one part patron, one part curator . . . [who] snub such traditional standards as age, provenance and investment value . . . practical people who want to touch and handle and, if possible, use their collections."

The Coadys were so taken with a fiddle-back mahogany chest of drawers in that show that they tracked down the artist, Jere Osgood, and commissioned him to make a wine cabinet: "our first piece of 'serious' furniture," as Judy now describes it. Over the next decade, they purchased or commissioned some

twenty-five more pieces, filling the historic Brooklyn Heights town house they then owned with the work of Judy Kensley McKie, Garry Knox Bennett, Ed Zucca, and other furniture artists for whom the Coady residence soon became a popular New York City stopping-off place.

One evening in 1980, the Coadys invited Garry Knox Bennett to dinner after the opening of an exhibition of his work, and Bennett brought along his gallery's owners, Warren Rubin and his wife, Bernice Wollman (page 122). From then until 1985, Judy served with Bernice as codirector of The Gallery at Workbench, organizing five major shows a year featuring furniture by both established and emerging artists. Some of these were landmark exhibitions, launching careers and, most importantly, bringing art/craft furniture to the attention of New York's design community.

Then, in 1985, Pat moved his investment business to Washington, D.C., where he is now U.S. executive director of the World

Garry Knox Bennett's 1978 "Bow-Wow, Cluck-Cluck" bench occupies stair landing that overlooks surrounding woodland. Bench is natural and dyed redwood with cherry edging on seat. OPPOSITE TOP Cedar outdoor chair by Jack Larimore, 1986. OPPOSITE BOTTOM The Coadys' first commissioned piece, a 1975 wine cabinet by Jere Osgood, is flanked by Alphonse Mattia's "City Boy" valet, purchased in 1985. Wine cabinet is hickory; valet is painted cherry and poplar with a tic-tac-toe board on the seat.

Bank. Judy's professional involvement in the contemporary crafts movement was temporarily curtailed. Given two weeks to find a house in the D.C. area, Judy chose a contemporary structure in a wooded setting that is "exactly the opposite of our row house in Brooklyn. I didn't want the children to have any basis for a comparison that would make them miss their former home."

One comparison that can be drawn, however, is the different ways in which the art/craft furniture collected by the Coadys over the past eighteen years interacts in its old and new settings. In Brooklyn Heights, the Coadys' principal pieces had a more formal, objectlike quality that made them seem quite special, in Northern Virginia, these same pieces take their places so quietly that they seem, at times, almost to merge with the environment. Judy prefers the latter because of natural correspondences: handmade furniture surrounded by trees; handmade clay close to the earth. "It's a more relaxed, casual atmosphere," says Judy, "and we discovered after we'd bought the house that the architect who designed it also makes his own furniture. Living with the vision of an architect who is concerned with furniture as an integral part of design seems right for us."

Now removed, geographically, from many artists whose work they admire, the Coadys are less likely to commission pieces than to buy from galleries or on the basis of slides sent to them. Judy admits that "it's not as much fun as seeing the work in progress and getting to know the artists," but she also points out that in the last few years contemporary craft furniture has become easily accessible nationwide. "This is no longer a regional phenomenon. There are good galleries springing up all over the country—St. Louis, Chicago, San Francisco, Los Angeles—you name it, and there's at least one dealer in the area who knows what's going on."

Of course, the Coadys themselves have had a lot to do with this broadening interest, but when people who have only recently discovered art/craft furniture tell them how lucky they are to have bought certain pieces while the artists were still relatively unknown, Judy is bemused. "Luck had nothing to do with it. We took chances when there was not a lot of agreement out there. To find what we wanted, we had to backpack our infants to once-a-year events like the New England Crafts Fair. In those days, there were only a few galleries, like The Elements in New York, that showed furniture."

No longer infants, the Coady children have definite opinions about what their parents collect. "Oh, the 'Japanese' look," sniffed the older daughter, Margaret, eyeing a recent acquisition, "if you've seen it once, you've seen it. Period." "The children do have very developed tastes," observes Judy, "even if they're not yet fully informed. One thing they have gotten out of all this, though, is a sense of what an artist is and how he or she is different from a business person or a politician. We think these are important distinctions to make early in life."

Peter Joseph's living room sums up the artistry of John Dunnigan, who was commissioned to make most of the furnishings, including the hand-tufted wool and silk "Jewel" rug (with Wendy Wahl, 1988) and the small etched sandblasted panels set into the lower portion of the window frames, part of the artist's 1988 "Metamorphosis" series. Couch, chairs, and ottoman are Dunnigan's 1985 "Biedermeier Suite," executed in pearwood and ebonized mahogany with silk upholstery; "Entasis" torchers are faux pear (cherry) with pink glass, 1986. The only pieces not by Dunnigan are Judy Kensley McKie's 1984 "Bird Table" of carved mahogany; and Wendell Castle's "Plantain" coffee table made of primavera, amaranth, and ebony, also 1984.

WITH COMFORT IN MIND

Cycling home from the beach one summer afternoon, Peter Joseph wandered into the Pritam & Eames Gallery in East Hampton and discovered the world of art/craft furniture. Over the next several years, he occasionally returned to the gallery, but not until he was about to move to Los Angeles did he introduce himself to the owners, Warren and Bebe Johnson. "I explained that I was relocating to the West Coast and probably would not be back to the gallery again. And I made them an offer for seven or eight pieces of furniture that were in the shop at the time." Those pieces promptly were shipped to Los Angeles, where Joseph found an apartment for them and settled down to what he recalls as "the tremendously satisfying experience of living with something you know has been specially created by another human being who has put an important part of himself or herself into it."

That was in 1981. Joseph subsequently returned to New York City, reestablished contact with Pritam & Eames, and got to know, personally, the artists whose work so pleased him. As his circle of artist acquaintances grew, he began commission-

ing special pieces while continuing to purchase for both his East Coast residence and a former home in Fort Worth, Texas. In 1987, he bought a Manhattan apartment and retained David M. Schwarz Architectural Services of Washington, D.C., to design it with the intention that it be furnished entirely with the work of craft artists. To accommodate his Fort Worth acquisitions, he subsequently bought an adjacent apartment on the same floor.

Joseph's collection today is not only one of the largest and finest in the country, it is also one of the most complete: Every piece of furniture, every decorative object in the Joseph apartment is handcrafted, most of them one-of-a-kind (as opposed to limited-edition) pieces. The rugs, the wood-inlay flooring, some small windowpanes, even the walls of one room have been designed by craft artists. Except for kitchen appliances and bathroom fixtures, there is

ABOVE AND OPPOSITE Wendell Castle's 1981 desk and chairs made of English curly sycamore with light pink stain, amaranth, and 8,500 pieces of ebony inlay. Slip seats are covered top and bottom in fabric by Jack Lenor Larsen. RIGHT Robert March's tall table in boire, 1986.

not a trace of commercial design or mass production.

The effect is stunning. Each individual piece has its own character, its own elaborately developed detail, yet, overall, a feeling of quiet harmony pervades. The use of light upholstery, predominantly light woods, light flooring, and light walls is a skillful ordering device. What ultimately makes the Joseph collection so satisfying, however, is its close focus: Only eight artists are represented in the principal rooms of the apartment and, of those eight, four —John Dunnigan, Richard Scott Newman, Judy McKie, and Wendell Castle—are dominant. Recurring motifs in these artists' work subtly tie together the many unique pieces, creating a visual coherence that is unusual in a collection of this size.

The true unifying force is Joseph himself, for whom collecting—and especially the commissioning process—is an outlet for creative urges that have been subordinated to a fast-paced investment career. While earning his Bachelor of Arts and Master of Public Administration degrees at Princeton, Joseph also studied sculpture with Jim Seawright, then the head of the University's visual-arts program. Now the chairman and CEO of Rosecliff, a New York investment company that manages the $1.4 billion assets of Acadia Partners Ltd., Joseph derives a special pleasure from working with the artists he collects.

"Playing an active role with people who are devoting their lives to an aesthetic ideal, and being able to participate with them in the design process, is terrifically

OPPOSITE *Details of Richard Scott Newman's and Castle's work. UPPER LEFT Newman's writing desk in curly cherry and ebony, 1984; and "Dream" chair in cherry with vermeil, 1982. UPPER RIGHT Wendell Castle's "Sub-Nine" end table in tulipwood and blue leather, 1984; BELOW Close-up of his "Plantain" coffee table; primavera, amaranth, and ebony. View from Joseph's library ABOVE shows silk-upholstered couch, chair, and ottoman commissioned of Wendy Stayman in 1988. Couch is steamed Swiss pearwood with ebony detail; chair and ottoman are ebony with bone detail. Visible in foyer at left in photo is Bruce Volz's 1985 "American Flyer I" cabinet; Pau amarillo, dyed veneer, walnut, brass, silk, and ceramic beads. Through doorway is Newman's writing desk and "Dream" chair.*

Castle's "Caligari" library wall was commissioned in 1988 to "free up the environment from its normal boundaries." Above irregular wainscoting of satinwood wedges, Castle placed tilting bookshelves in wall of fragmented doughnut shapes formed in gesso with acrylic paint. A black leather-covered shelf separates gesso wall from satinwood wainscoting. Rug pattern, "WJ" by Dunnigan/Wahl, picks up angularity of room, to which Wendy Stayman's couch, chair, and ottoman restore visual order. Centered in room is Judy Kensley McKie's "Chase" table; bronze and glass, 1987.

exciting. I like the idea of nourishing their talents, of allowing them to go a step further in their art." A good example of this is a recently purchased Judy Kensley McKie bed. "I knew Judy had a show coming up and, needing a bed, I asked her to make one for the show. I really didn't give her any direction, but I loved what she did and I bought it." As in this instance with McKie, Joseph often gives free rein to the artists he commissions, but what he finds particularly interesting is their willingness to incorporate into their work a patron's point of view: "I adjust and they adjust; it's a shared learning process."

One result of the sharing process to which Joseph alludes is the distinctly livable quality of his collection. "This is my home. I live here, I work here, I entertain friends here." Friends visiting for the first time may worry that they have arrived at a museum, but, according to Joseph, they quickly get comfortable. What happens if a guest spills something on one of his favorite pieces? "It's not a great feeling," admits Joseph, "but I keep lots of cleaners handy. And if there's any real damage, the artist usually shares my concern and will cooperate in repairing it." In fact, the livability—as well as the aesthetic stimulation —of Joseph's art/craft furnishings has inspired some of his friends to start collecting for their own homes.

The latest room to be completed in the Joseph apartment is the library, for which Wendell Castle was commissioned to create an unusual wall system, the startling irregularity of which is heightened by the pattern of the John Dunnigan rug on the floor. The much more sober couch, armchair, and ottoman by Wendy Stayman were designed specifically to rebalance the room, in which Joseph also has placed Judy Kensley McKie's whimsical "Chase" table. Having seen another library wall executed by Castle in lacewood (page 54), Joseph concluded that to enclose his library entirely in woodwork would be "too confining." Therefore, he urged Castle toward what Joseph describes as the "anarchic" combination of a plaster and colored wall, with whole and fragmented "doughnut" shapes above a wainscoting of satinwood wedges. These two elements are divided by a black leather shelf that describes an erratic line picked up in the bold angularity of the carpet design, then reinforced by Castle's quirky tilting bookshelves. Joseph, who claims one becomes accustomed to the tilt, likes the off-balance character of his library because it "frees up the environment from its normal boundaries. This room has a warm, textured feeling that I really love."

Although it is only recently that Joseph has begun to collect Castle, he owns several signature pieces from different periods in Castle's constantly evolving career. The umbrella stand is a prized example of Castle's trompe l'oeil period, ca. 1977; the 1981 lady's writing desk and chairs represent Castle at what Joseph believes was "the moment he was defining himself as a maker of fine furniture before moving on to more sculptural work"; the 1984 end table supported by a massing of

LEFT *Wendell Castle's 1977 trompe l'oeil mahogany "Umbrella Stand with Umbrella" DETAIL OPPOSITE performs its normal function in Joseph's entrance foyer, behind which is visible Bruce Volz's "American Flyer I" cabinet. BELOW Volz's 1984 tall clock (wenge, dyed veneer, mother-of-pearl, brass, eggshell, holly, and abalone), which terminates hallway carpeted in John Dunnigan/Wendy Wahl's "Golden Section" rug, 1988.*

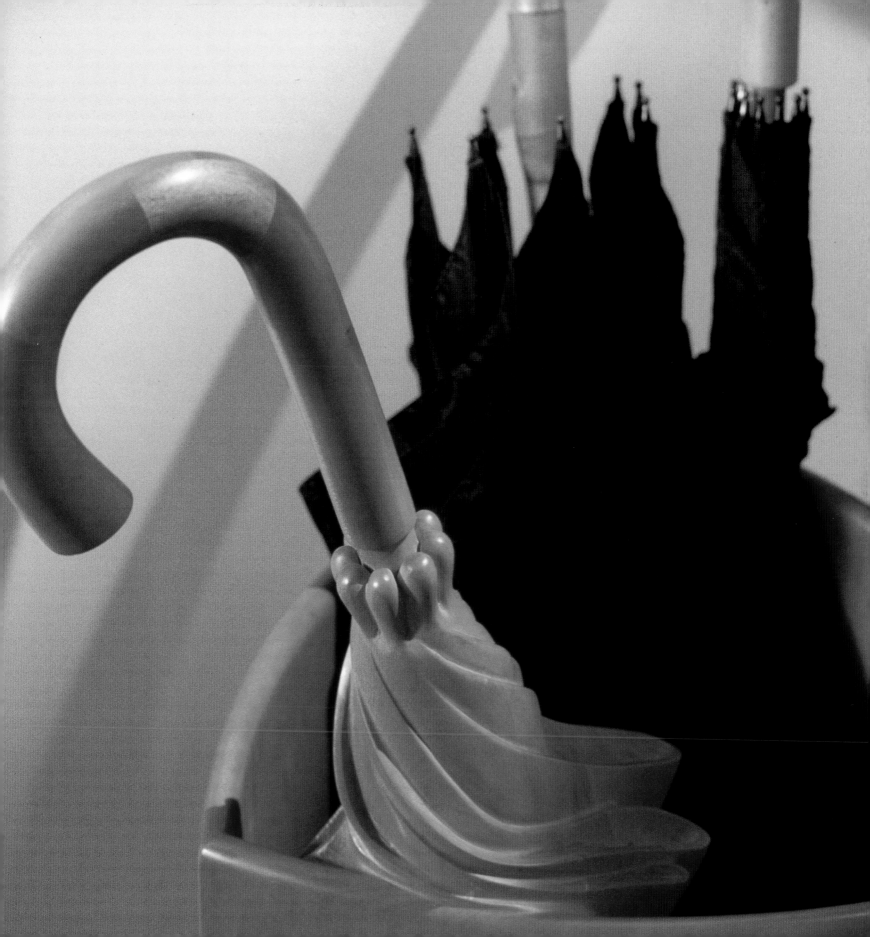

blue cones is typical of Castle's Postmodern period; and the 1988 library is clearly the work of Castle as sculptor.

It is, in part, the ongoing development in Castle's aesthetic that attracts Joseph to his work, while with John Dunnigan—who is represented in Joseph's apartment by everything from couches, tables, chairs, and a desk to torchers, rugs, and windowpanes—it is this artist's "creativity and flexibility" that Joseph values. The "warmth" and "neoclassicism" of Richard Scott Newman are also very appealing to Joseph, and he finds that Judy McKie's "light, primitive style" provides a refreshing contrast to the rest of his collection. Despite his tendency to concentrate on these and a few other artists (Bruce Volz is well represented in his apartment, and more pieces by Volz, Jere Osgood, and Tim Philbrick are on their way from Joseph's former Fort Worth home), Joseph does not limit the scope of his purchases. "I buy what I like," says Joseph, "including the work of younger, lesser-known artists whom I think I might help with a significant commission."

For Joseph, collecting art/craft furniture is more than a hobby; it is a serious exploration of his own aesthetic impulses. The reward he seeks is not the thrill of acquisition or the achievement of some critical mass. "What pleases me most," says Joseph, "is sitting down to a desk that is one of a kind—a statement of everything that the artist believed in at the time—and knowing that that artist put everything he or she had into it."

Joseph's dining room is furnished with Judy Kensley McKie's "Table with Grinning Beasts," "Carved Bird" cabinet, and John Dunnigan's "Tardis" chairs and "Jungle" rug. Table is bleached maple, 1987; cabinet is lime wood with rosa Portugal marble, 1985; chairs are bleached maple with Wendy Wahl upholstery, 1988. To left of dining room is McKie's tall cabinet; lime wood and milk paint, 1987; and, in entrance foyer, Albert Paley's forged and fabricated mild-steel plant stand, 1981.

Details of Judy Kensley McKie's "Carved Bird" cabinet OPPOSITE, tall cabinet BELOW, and "Dragonfly" chest of drawers RIGHT reveal the animation and "light, primitive style" that make this artist's work so appealing to Joseph. "Dragonfly" chest is carved lime wood, 1987.

MANHATTAN PIED-A-TERRE

Known throughout the world for his own craft—that of Muppet making—artist/writer/producer/director Jim Henson is also a devotee of craft furnishings, both antique and contemporary. "I love what's going on now in the craft movement," says Henson. "Perhaps that's because many of the people I work with—costumers, prop makers, jewelry makers—are craftspeople. But I also think there's much more warmth, much more skill and intensity in craft today than in much of the painting and sculpture that's been produced over the last twenty years."

Given such predilections, it is not surprising that, in 1983, when he acquired a Manhattan pied-à-terre for himself and his five grown children, Henson insisted that it be designed "with craft and for craft, but not as a showplace or a museum. This is a place to live and work and see people." To accommodate this ambitious program in a relatively compact space that had the pleasant but undistinguished details typical of apartments built in the 1920s, architect Anthony Tsirantonakis first divided the long narrow living room into three parterres. These platforms step up toward magnificent views across Central Park, allowing for a clear distinction of activities: dining and desk work on the first or ground level; formal display of Henson's wide-ranging collection of art and memorabilia on the second; and on the third or highest parterre, seating that overlooks the park or can be oriented to professionally engineered audio-video equipment.

To reinforce these changes in elevation, Tsirantonakis introduced custom-designed display cases and freestanding columns at either side of the middle parterre, and on the third, large custom-designed cabinets to house the audio-video equipment. A custom-designed couch centered on two more freestanding columns forms a low wall between the second and third levels. Within this architectural container, a number of artists and craftspeople were set to

"Muppeteer" Jim Henson's Manhattan apartment, for which he commissioned sculptor Patsy Norvell to create etched glass doors (shown closed, LEFT) opening onto multilevel living room. Visible within are one of a pair of three-legged side chairs by Wendell Castle and Judy Kensley McKie's "Jungle" dining table, chairs, and "Turtle" bench.

Detail of John Kahn's wood floor on second parterre OPPOSITE shows one of Patsy Norvell's three etched glass insets illuminated from below. RIGHT Bright-eyed creature peeks around from back of one of Judy Kensley McKie's four dining chairs.

Back of custom-designed couch ABOVE acts as
low wall dividing second and third parterres,
providing backdrop for Judy Kensley McKie's
"Turtle" bench; carved and painted mahogany,
1983. Perched on top of bench is "Turtle" bowl
by McKie. Her carved, stained, and painted
mahogany "Lizard" plant stand, 1983, guards
rise to third parterre. RIGHT McKie's "Jungle"
dining table and chairs; carved, stained,
painted, and natural-finish butternut, 1984.
OPPOSITE Sam Maloof's bench, commissioned
by Henson in 1988, and a decorative metal
panel from Selfridges department store, London.
Serpent-entwined floor lamp was made by Edgar
Brandt in the 1920s.

work, creating floors, light fixtures, doors, and furnishings. Purchases out of contemporary craft galleries and a few antiques —principally Art Nouveau, the forms and lines of which Henson finds suggestive of the organic curves in pieces such as Wendell Castle's "Crescent" rocker—complete the remarkably eclectic mix.

The overall effect, however, is one of quiet relaxation. As Henson observes, "it's the sense of detail, the ornament, that ties it all together"—that and the fact that the architect was able to separate the multiple purposes of the room without interrupting the visual sweep toward the park views. For doors opening onto the living rooms from the entry hall, Henson, Tsirantonakis, and associate architect Anne Manning commissioned sculptor Patsy Norvell to create clear glass panels etched in delicate plant forms. Then, for the second parterre, sculptor John Kahn was commissioned to design a wood floor inset with layered glass etched by Norvell. When lit from below (the elevation of the parterre allows underlighting), Norvell's flowers appear to float in bottomless pools. Pools of light also appear on the ceiling, thrown from the tops of the columns, for which glassmaker Christopher Cosma blew bowl-shaped fixtures. The far wall of the third parterre is illuminated by a pair of sconces handblown by Cosma.

For the first, or dining, parterre, Judy Kensley McKie was commissioned to make a table and four chairs, which she carved with twining vines, peeking birds, creeping lizards, and other whimsical creatures.

Three additional McKie pieces purchased from galleries—a bench in the shape of a turtle poised on exaggerated legs, a small carved turtle bowl, and a lizard plant stand —complete the menagerie. Less figurative pieces, such as Wendell Castle's "Crescent" rocker, his "Three-Legged" side chairs, and a Sam Maloof rocker, also were purchased; and for one of the bedrooms, Wendy Stayman was commissioned in 1985 to design and make a pair of night tables (not shown).

"I enjoy the commissioning process," says Henson, "and if I ever furnish another house, I would like to have more things made. But commissioning can be a bit tricky. When you see a piece that you love in a gallery, at least you know what you're

getting. A couple of times I have had to abandon a commission in the middle of design."

Although he claims that he is not building an art/craft furniture collection, Henson still continues to buy for his Manhattan apartment; for example, the recently acquired Sam Maloof bench that now sits handsomely in front of a decorative metal panel originally installed in Selfridges department store, London (other panels like it are now in the Victoria and Albert Museum and the Brighton Museum).

"What I like best are craft pieces that I can use, not the sort of thing I have to put on a shelf. When craft moves away from function in order to be 'high art,' I lose interest in it."

ABOVE LEFT AND DETAIL OPPOSITE Sam Maloof rocker in master bedroom is flanked by Louis Comfort Tiffany floor lamp. In guest bedroom ABOVE CENTER Wendell Castle's "Crescent" rocker, one of a series of twenty made late 1970s to early 1980s, sits next to Wendy Stayman's side table. Castle's three-legged side chair of cherry wood, 1979, is used with custom-designed worktable built into rear wall of multipurpose living room ABOVE RIGHT.

WEEKENDS IN THE VILLAGE

"We walk in the door late on Friday nights and it's like finding a lot of old friends already gathered to greet us." That's the way this two-career family describes the art/craft furniture that they've bought, commissioned, or moved from the city to their weekend house. "The most remarkable thing about these pieces is how, despite their aesthetic differences, they live so happily together. In fact, they bring a kind of order to the chaos we thought would result when we first arrived here with all our 'leftovers' and yard-sale specials."

Typical of many older houses in the villages of Long Island's South Shore, this 1917 Colonial Revival house has rather small rooms, and it is because the rooms are so small that pieces such as Robert

Steven Whittelsey's 1982 cupboard is crafted in "found" wood with paints and finishes left as found. Shape of upper doors reveals origins as wheelbarrow sides.

Whitley's rocker dominate an otherwise eclectic environment. Similarly, Judy Mc-Kie's animal plant stands have a presence that is much larger than their actual dimensions. For all their "importance," however, these pieces do not enjoy special status. "Judy [McKie] would die if she saw the water running out the bottom of our ferns." Not even two young sons, often wet and sandy, have so far managed to damage any of the art/craft furniture, one piece of which—the Steven Whittelsey cupboard— is used by the older boy to store everything from (usually dirty) clothes and sporting equipment to his butterfly collection.

"We like buying and commissioning these things because it gives us an opportunity to patronize the living arts—and living artists. In fact, we regard much of the hand-made furniture being produced now as more appealing than most of what passes for 'fine' art today. Well-crafted furniture, such as Robert Whitley's work, has a strength and integrity that makes it ageless. We expect to pass these things on to our grandchildren, maybe even our great-grandchildren."

Garry Knox Bennett's 1982 "Checkerboard" bench in redwood and dyed poplar ABOVE is none the worse for wear after years of sitting just inside door of ski house where family once used it to change boots. Robert Whitley's rocker FAR LEFT was made in black walnut in 1984 from a 1953 design. "This is the most comfortable chair I've ever sat in," claims the owner, who commissioned a second one for his office. "There is a sensual quality to the curve of the arms that is undeniably agreeable." LEFT AND OPPOSITE Judy McKie's "Snake" plant stand; painted wood, 1983.

Deck of Lewis home overlooks unspoiled hills of adjoining parkland, a perfect setting for Garry Knox Bennett's bench; galvanized steel, redwood, and fir, 1980.

A FAMILY TRADITION

After he retired from his position at family-owned Best Products Company several years ago, Andy Lewis and his wife, Ginny, left Richmond, Virginia, to settle in the hills north of Berkeley, California. While Andy pursues his Ph.D. in mathematics, he and Ginny are building a collection of art/craft furniture that spans two decades—from Robert Whitley pieces made in the 1960s to recent work by Garry Knox Bennett, Jack Larimore, and Ed Zucca.

It is, in fact, the second generation of a legendary collection. Andy's parents, Sidney and Frances Lewis, are among the earliest and most influential patrons of the new craft movement in America. When he built a new headquarters for Best Products in 1979, chairman Sidney Lewis commis-

Dining table ABOVE is by Bennett; bamboo and California walnut, with California live-oak top, 1981. Chair is by Ed Zucca; figured maple with Shaker seat webbing, 1975. Sideboard is also by Zucca; walnut, maple, and glass with ebony and ivory pull, 1978. ABOVE RIGHT Detail of Bennett's desk; walnut, yellow satinwood, and wenge with metal fittings, bone, and faux tortoiseshell pulls, 1984.

sioned furniture artist Ed Zucca to make the boardroom table—a spirited departure from the usually conservative approach to corporate furnishings.

In 1985, the Lewises, along with Mr. and Mrs. Paul Mellon, endowed the new west wing of the Virginia Museum of Fine Arts in Richmond, and the Lewises donated more than eight hundred paintings, sculp-

tures, decorative objects, and furnishings, including some important Art Nouveau and Art Deco pieces. To replace the furniture given to the museum, the senior Lewises are now amassing what is probably going to be the largest and finest private collection of twentieth-century furniture in the United States, if not in the world. Included will be work by many of the artists

already represented in Andy and Ginny's collection: pieces by Wendell Castle, Judy Kensley McKie, John Makepeace, and most of the other prominent contemporary woodworkers; and the best examples of furniture designed by artists and architects like Dakota Jackson, Forest Myers, Ettore Sottsass, and Robert Venturi.

The spirit of the younger Lewises' collection is relaxed, intimate, and very much in keeping with their casual life-style. One of their pieces houses another major collection: handmade jewelry from all over the world. "For us, collecting is a way of life, a constant learning process, and an endless source of pleasure. The fact that we can use what we collect makes it all that much more satisfying."

ABOVE LEFT Flanking arm of architect Michael Graves's couch are Bob Trotman's "Dancing" end tables; maple and mahogany with lacquered designs, 1981. Stained glass door by Narcissus Quagliata DETAIL ABOVE RIGHT was installed 1984.

THE ART OF ENTERTAINING

To every confirmed collector there comes a moment when the question of what to buy is eclipsed by the problem of where to put it. Even the largest houses and apartments have a finite amount of wall and floor space. Sadly, new acquisitions and old favorites are relegated to basements, attics, or climate-controlled warehouses. Occasionally, pieces are rotated in and out of storage or sold off to reduce the surplus. Eventually, they may be rescued by surprised heirs or deposited in museums to which can fall the tricky job of cataloguing life-time collections documented only by tattered, nondescriptive sales receipts.

Not so in the case of Anne and Ronald Abramson, who are amassing one of the largest and finest collections of craft furniture in the country. Their approach has been much bolder: Furnish a suburban house with craft pieces, live in it, and, when it's full, buy an apartment designed specifically as an environment for art. When that apartment is full, too, buy another in the same building. In short, the Abramsons have built their own live-in museum: entrance foyer, living room, dining room, kitchen, numerous bedrooms, even closets

Barrel-vaulted foyer of Abramson apartment is furnished with chairs, table, and couch by Charles Crowley, pair of chairs at rear by Todd White, and hall table by Wendell Castle. Sculpture hanging on far wall is by glass artist Dan Dailey.

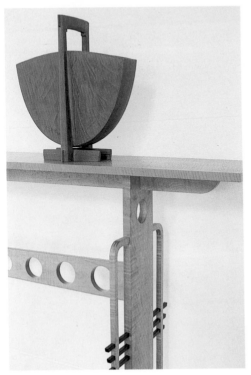

Abramson living room ABOVE LEFT is centered by Rosanne Somerson's couch and "Radiator" coffee table DETAIL LEFT, about which are grouped chairs (counterclockwise from rear) by Peter Dean, Jay Stanger, and Vickie Moss. In left-hand corner is "Madonna" tall clock by Peter Pierobon. Flanking windows are Dan Dailey's "Etrus" tripods and John Dunnigan's floor lamp. Against right-hand wall is Ed Zucca's console, shown in detail FAR LEFT with Michael Hurwitz's wooden vessel. ABOVE Ed Zucca's "Time Is Money" clock, with Wendell Castle's hall table in background. Close-up view of Jay Stanger's wood-flooring inlay OPPOSITE reveals playful interaction with legs of Dailey's tripods.

intended principally to accommodate handmade furniture.

"We use the first apartment for weekends in the city and for entertaining," Ron explains, "the second apartment will be for guests." Understandably the atmosphere is more gallerylike than residential, but not even the largest gallery could display the best work of more than two dozen top craft artists so extensively or so seductively.

"Everything in the apartment is handmade," according to Ron, "even the wood floor," which was inlaid by Jay Stanger. The wood inlay, used throughout the public spaces, was Anne's choice, a kind of reverse trompe l'oeil alternative to carpeting (usually it is carpeting that is woven to mimic inlaid-wood or stone-floor patterning). The bedroom carpeting, although not custom designed, is by noted textile artist Jack Lenor Larsen. Even the accessories, including many of the dishes, plates, and cups, are the work of craft artists.

The setting for this stunning collection is an interior designed by David M. Schwarz Architectural Services to function equally well as both living and display space. Carefully controlled to allow the individual works of art and craft to speak for themselves, the space nonetheless makes its own rather powerful design statement. Be-

In his "Time Is Money" tall clock OPPOSITE, Zucca makes visual pun through lamination of his own cancelled checks and genuine U.S. one-dollar bills over entire surface, using dimes and quarters to mark hours on face. RIGHT Detail of Castle's "The Midnight Marriage" hall table; ebonized cherry, ebonized walnut, and yellow analine-dyed curly maple, 1986.

cause the apartment was purchased while the building was still under construction, it was possible to achieve special modifications such as the skylighted barrel vault, gabled ceilings, and high oculus windows. The resulting volumetric quality of the space, emphasized by cove lighting under the gables, is strong enough to counter the force of the objects in it, thus stabilizing the furniture without overwhelming it.

In the kitchen, a diagonal inlay of black vinyl floor tiles beneath a serving island plays off the gabled ceilings and triangularly shaped foyer, introducing an asymmetry that perfectly complements craft

artist Charles Mark's stools. Although Schwarz claims that none of the spaces was designed specifically to accommodate a particular artist or piece of furniture, it is difficult to imagine Mark's stools anywhere but in this room, on this floor.

Ron, a Washington, D.C., attorney, and Anne, who publishes *Museum & Arts* magazine, work as partners in assembling their collection. And, like other collectors, they know many of the craft artists whose pieces they've purchased or commissioned, often inviting them to stay in the apartment that has been dedicated to their work. "Our approach is to follow an

Abramson dining chairs and table ABOVE were made by Ed Zucca in 1987. Chairs are bleached curly maple and anodized aluminum with Jack Lenor Larsen upholstery fabric; table is bleached curly maple, ebony, and Honduras mahogany. OPPOSITE Kitchen stools by Charles Mark, 1987.

Bedrooms are no less rich in art/craft furnishings than the Abramson's more formal public spaces. Even closets reveal such delights as John Cedarquist's mirror LEFT, in which is reflected chair by renowned English furniture maker John Makepeace. Other choice pieces found in bedrooms are Tom Hucker's award-winning bronze and wenge low table DETAIL BELOW and three of Alphonse Mattia's well-known valets OPPOSITE: "Mr. Potato-Head"; bleached oak and sycamore, dyed and painted, 1984; "Knothead"; ebonized walnut and sycamore, 1984; and "Architect's Valet"; painted wood, 1985.

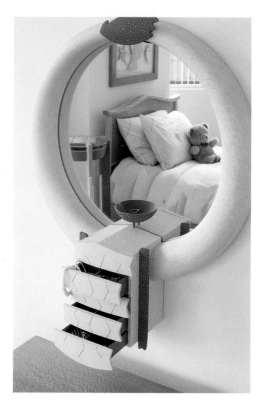

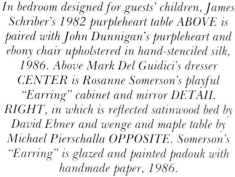

In bedroom designed for guests' children, James Schriber's 1982 purpleheart table ABOVE is paired with John Dunnigan's purpleheart and ebony chair upholstered in hand-stenciled silk, 1986. Above Mark Del Guidici's dresser CENTER is Rosanne Somerson's playful "Earring" cabinet and mirror DETAIL RIGHT, in which is reflected satinwood bed by David Ebner and wenge and maple table by Michael Pierschalla OPPOSITE. Somerson's "Earring" is glazed and painted padouk with handmade paper, 1986.

artist's career and purchase pieces from each succeeding phase of his or her work," says Ron, who is a trustee of the American Craft Council and a member of the Board of Commissioners of the Renwick Gallery.

The Abramsons date their interest in craft to 1978, when they began purchasing art glass. By 1980, they had bought their first piece of furniture: a mirror by Alphonse Mattia. Since then, about two-thirds of their acquisitions have been purchased ("we buy in spurts") and one-third are commissions. Although they continue to collect actively, they consider this apartment to be complete: "complete, but not static; we do move things about and make substitutions from time to time." The second apartment is being furnished with

craft pieces, too; so, for the moment, there's no problem of where to put it.

There remains, however, the question of why. What is it that compels collectors like the Abramsons to continue acquiring without deaccessioning, even if it means building additional "homes" for their art? "We feel quite fortunate that we live in a time when handmade furniture is achieving the public and private attention that it deserves," explains Ron, "and we feel privileged to know so many of the amazingly talented people who make it. Our goal is to applaud that talent, to celebrate the extraordinarily high level of art and craftsmanship that exists in America today." Stepping into the Abramsons' apartment, one can virtually hear that applause.

*Detail of Mark Del Guidici's post-modernist
dresser; painted maple with gold leafing,
Australian lacewood veneer top, painted maple
pulls, and brass rods, 1985. OPPOSITE Detail
of Ron Puckett's 1986 wenge and lacewood
writing table paired with Kalle Fauset's "Moon"
chair; holly, bloodwood, purpleheart, and
ebonized walnut, 1984.*

GROWING UP IN SOHO

He's an interior construction company executive with a degree in architecture and she's a weaver who also directs a criminal justice program at a major university. Like many of their contemporaries, this young couple had always thought of furniture in terms of classic "designer" pieces. However, exposure to the crafts movement during their college days led to encounters in the early 1980s with people like Rick and Ruth Snyderman of the Snyderman Gallery in Philadelphia, and Judy Coady (The Gallery at Workbench, New York). Then, when they moved to New York City in 1982 and began to furnish a newly renovated SoHo loft, they discovered that commissioning one-of-a-kind pieces could cost no more than buying the kind of good contract furniture that they had always wanted.

Beginning with a Rosanne Somerson couch that was two and a half years in the making, the couple has commissioned a

Centerpiece of loft living area is Rosanne Somerson's couch in leather with white-stained wood cutouts applied to frame of ebonized wood and purpleheart, 1986. Dale Broholm chair is pearwood and lacquered wood with fabric upholstery, 1986. Carl Andree Davidt floor lamp, entitled "Green Cloud Caution Marker," combines cast, stainless, and painted steel with brass and etched glass, 1984.

new work almost every year, often as gifts to one another or to mark special occasions. "By the time Rosanne's couch arrived, we had already bought a Garry Knox Bennett desk with my first bonus, and I had commissioned Carl Andree Davidt to make a floor lamp as a birthday present to my wife." The lamp wasn't quite finished in time for the surprise party, so Davidt substituted a colored pencil sketch that the couple still treasures as a memento of their early adventures in collecting.

When their first son was born in 1986, the eager parents looked all over the country for children's furniture in production, hoping to find something creative. After waiting nine months for delivery from a commercial manufacturer in Texas ("it was taking longer than having the baby"), they saw a table and chair set made by their friend Joanne Sheemas and canceled the other order. Similarly, the search for an upholstered lounge chair that would "make a design statement but still be comfortable to sit on" led them to Dale Broholm, who enlarged the scale of a piece he had already designed and changed the color to meet the couple's specifications.

As their family grows (a second child was born in 1989), the goal is to keep on collecting, but with an eye to functional requirements as well as price. "We go to a lot of craft shows and we look for young, undiscovered artists. Living in limited space on a limited budget means we have to make every piece count."

Garry Knox Bennett desk OPPOSITE TOP has glass top with painted edges supported by dyed walnut and cocobola legs and aluminum tressle, 1984. Lacquered wood child's table and chairs OPPOSITE BOTTOM, DETAIL LEFT are by Joanne Sheemas. BELOW High kitchen chairs in stained wood, commissioned from Ken Strickland in 1982.

BROOKLYN NEIGHBORS

It was quite by accident that neighboring residents in a Brooklyn Heights co-op discovered their common interest in art/craft furniture. When the rambunctious children of one family ruined the caning of a settee stationed by the other in an elevator lobby serving the two apartments, the owner of the disheveled piece commissioned Wendy Stayman to make a settee that not only would be indestructible but would match a hall table that the children's parents had purchased out of Stayman's first show in 1982. Only then did the embarrassed parents learn that their neighbor was one of the earliest and most devoted collectors of fine handcrafted furniture in the United States.

"I don't think of myself as a collector," protests the neighbor. "I bought my first piece in 1965 because I needed it to

Jere Osgood dining table was commissioned in 1966, his curly maple sideboard in 1974, and cherry chairs in 1975. Geoffrey Warner screen RIGHT was purchased in 1988.

White oak and marquetry "Winter" cabinet
LEFT, DETAIL BELOW was made in 1983
by Zivko Radenkov, a student of James Krenov.
Michael Hurwitz's 1981 console UPPER
RIGHT is zebrawood with rosewood drawer
pull DETAIL OPPOSITE. Lamp table
CENTER AND LOWER RIGHT is 1987 Jere
Osgood commission, executed in pearwood and
curly maple.

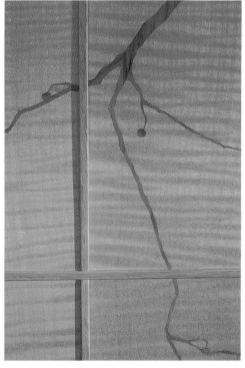

furnish my apartment. I was shopping for pots or weavings in America House [a now-defunct craft gallery once located near the old American Craft Museum] and up on the second floor, where it was about 150 degrees, I found a chest of drawers by Jere Osgood. It was just the size and shape I had been looking for, so I bought it. Then Jere called, saying he hadn't expected to sell it and could he borrow it back for a show? I said yes, provided he would put me on the top of his list to make a dining room table."

Thus began a friendship between patron and artist that has spanned more than twenty years and eight major acquisitions, resulting in what is probably the largest collection of Osgood's work in the country. Significantly, all but one of these acquisitions have been commissioned. (Osgood, who is best known for his tapered lamination and compound bending techniques, only occasionally accepts commissions.) The exception is the chair shown above. "Jere was delivering the dining room chairs I had commissioned when I happened to look out the window and there, on the pavement below, was our old doorman making himself comfortable in a swell-looking armchair that had come off

OPPOSITE Upholstered corner chair with maple frame, made in 1965, and cherry dictionary cabinet, commissioned in 1977, are two of eight major acquisitions from Osgood. Wendy Stayman's cherry, curly maple, and ebony veneer settee was commissioned in 1983 after neighbors purchased hall table in 1982. Mirror over table was commissioned of Stayman in 1984 to complete furnishing of shared lobby.

the truck. I told Jere to bring it up for a closer look, and here it stayed."

It is the "simple, unpretentious beauty" of handmade furniture that appeals to this collector, whose acquisitions, in addition to Osgood and Stayman, include works by Michael Hurwitz, Geoffrey Warner, and Zivko Radenkov, a student of James Krenov. Commercially made furnishings continue to be replaced by art/craft pieces,

but the favorite is still Osgood's dining room table. "The legs are so nice to feel. It's the tactile as well as the visual quality of these pieces that makes them so wonderful to live with."

The neighbors' children agree. They still drop soggy gloves on Wendy Stayman's furniture in the shared lobby, but Stayman faithfully returns to repair the damage. Good benches make good neighbors.

WOODLAND RETREAT

Out on the eastern end of Long Island, the only house sites with more caché than beach frontage are those so deeply secluded in pine forest that one can go for days without being invited to a cocktail party or seeing a pair of Gucci shoes. Inside one such retreat, there is a James Krenov cabinet that opens to reveal the treasures of hard-won solitude: a few shells, a well-preserved polyphemus moth, and a twisted bit of dry vine. The owner came upon the cabinet in much the same way that the moth and shells were discovered: through enduring passion rewarded by pure chance.

"I knew this cabinet by heart from a photograph," reminisces the owner. "I could sit and look at it all day. I was in love with it. Then, all of a sudden, it appeared at the Pritam & Eames Gallery [located in nearby East Hampton]. Of course, I had to have it." This kind of commitment to fine woodworking is rare, even among collectors, and everything about the owner's simple 1960s "cottage" speaks to that commitment. Warm polished wood floors and plain white walls are a perfect accompaniment for the choice craft furnishings that have been acquired over the years. The Krenov cabinet, a Judy Kensley McKie sideboard, and a Hank Gilpin table (with chairs by Hans Wegner) seem to have been specially made to sit in the tree-

Classic Hans Wegner chairs RIGHT complement Hank Gilpin's cherry dining table, purchased in 1982.

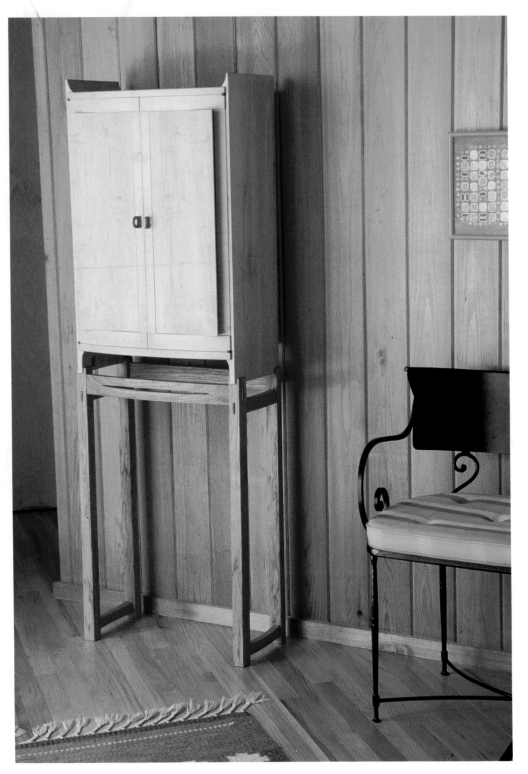

filtered sunlight that fills an undivided flow of living and dining space.

In fact, none of these pieces was commissioned. All were purchased and, as is so often the case, the slow, patient process of collecting has forged enduring friendships with the artists themselves. "What is nice about getting to know these people," explains the owner, "is that they all know each other and they get along so well." The same can be said of their furniture, especially as it has come together in the tranquility of this woodland retreat.

Doors of James Krenov's tall cabinet LEFT open to reveal display shelves and two shallow drawers with exquisitely carved pulls OPPOSITE. Cabinet, purchased 1983, is made of spalted maple, red oak, and partridge wood. ABOVE Judy Kensley McKie's carved lime wood sideboard, purchased 1984.

MISSION ACCOMPLISHED

One of the most potent forces in popularizing the contemporary crafts movement—that is, bringing it to people other than connoisseurs and collectors—was The Gallery at Workbench in New York City. During its eight years of operation (from 1980 to 1988), The Gallery mounted forty exhibitions of handmade furniture in which the work of some 130 students, emerging artists, and master craftsmen was showcased

in a commercial setting. These exhibitions were themed to explore contemporary woodworking from almost every angle. For example, in 1982 "Women Are Woodworking" made the point that, in a traditionally male-dominated field, some of the best—and most original—work is being done by women.

Founding director Bernice Wollman recalls that when she and her husband, War-

ren Rubin, opened The Gallery, "there really was no other place that provided steady representation for furniture artists. Occasionally, the craft galleries would mount small furniture shows, but they just didn't have the space to make it part of their regular business." In fact, for the first four years of its existence, The Gallery was not a business either, but a nonprofit information exchange where shoppers and, eventually, architects could purchase or commission pieces for the cost of the artists' time and materials. Not until a number of other craft-furniture galleries had been successfully established—in response to growing public interest—did Wollman and codirector Judy Coady (page 60) begin to charge a fee for The Gallery's services.

"We didn't want to be competing unfairly," explains Wollman, who first discovered craft furniture when she was introduced to West Coast artist Garry Knox Bennett in 1979. Her husband, Warren, with whom she is a partner in the sixty-store Workbench chain that he started back in 1955, asked Bennett to make all the furniture for his office. "Garry's shop was full of pieces that hadn't been sold, so

OPPOSITE *Living room of Wollman–Rubin country house with Judy Kensley McKie's glass-topped "Dog Eat Dog" table, one of six made in milk-painted wood, 1986. Wall-hung cabinet is Tommy Simpson's "Howdy House Before," 1984. Walnut and mixed-wood cabinet was made as jewel box, with shelves arrayed with toys and found objects and drawers filled with sand. In left-hand corner is Kristina Madsen's backgammon table and two chairs, exhibited in "Women Are Woodworking" at The Gallery at Workbench, 1982. Materials are bubinga, pearwood, ebony, and leather.*

Shown here is a detail of the mantelpiece and stereo cabinet installation designed by Ed Zucca for the Wollman–Rubin Manhattan apartment; fiddleback mahogany, satinwood, and ebony, 1988. OPPOSITE James Schriber's dresser and mirror, part of a commissioned suite of bedroom furniture completed in 1988. Wood is bird's-eye maple; dresser top is Avonite, a man-made material that looks like gray granite.

when it came time to ship Warren's furniture, we told him to load up the truck." An unimposing corner in the lower level of the Manhattan store was cleared (of the modestly priced but well-designed commercial furniture that is the Workbench stock-in-trade) and, with Bennett's powerful wood-and-metal pieces installed, The Gallery was launched.

In March 1988—some thirty-nine exhibitions later—The Gallery closed. "We felt our mandate had been fulfilled," says Wollman. "We set out to create a commercial market for these remarkable artists, and when they got to be so busy that they could no longer meet our show deadlines, we realized our mission had been accomplished." However, Wollman's and Rubin's personal commitment to the movement continues. "We always ran The Gallery on the strength of our personal interest," says Wollman, "and when The Gallery closed, we began commissioning for ourselves."

Recently, they've installed a bedroom suite by James Schriber and a mantelpiece and stereo cabinets by Ed Zucca in their Central Park West apartment. For an addition to their western Connecticut home, ceramacist Elizabeth MacDonald has tiled a floor-to-ceiling fireplace wall (see page 186) and metalworker Dimitri Gerakaris is making a small gate. "We've never considered ourselves collectors because we don't accumulate pieces for their own sake; for us, the main concern is, how does this fit in our lives?" A modest ambition, perhaps, but true to the spirit of The Gallery.

THE ARTIST AS COLLECTOR

Garry Knox Bennett is one of the foremost furniture makers at work today. His sometimes controversial but always distinctive pieces can be found in just about every major private collection and in several museums. Now he and his wife, Sylvia, who makes jewelry, are also being recognized as curators, having assembled—sometimes through swaps, borrowing, or as gifts from their furniture-maker friends, but mostly through purchases—a formidable collection of their own.

The Bennetts' large Victorian house, bought some twenty years ago in Ala-

In the Bennetts' Victorian house examples of Garry's and his friends' work mix happily. In foreground are Bennett's "African" chair; Honduras rosewood and assorted beads, 1986; and Judy Kensley McKie's carved and painted wood "Snake" table, 1988. Through the doorway are visible McKie's glass-topped, cast bronze "Chase" table, 1986, and Norman Petersen's "Ball and Cone" chair; purpleheart with gold- and silver-leafed wood and upholstery by K. Lee Manuel, 1985. Vase of flowers is sitting on molded plastic end table made by Wendell Castle in the mid-sixties. Ceiling-hung light fixture is gold- and silver-plated brass and copper, made by Garry in 1970 before he turned to furniture making. Love seat in bay window is an antique covered in black and white Op Art fabric by Brigette Riley.

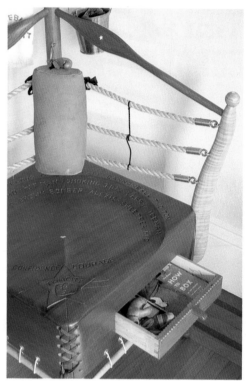

meda, California, where they were both born and raised, is filled with the cumulative evidence of Garry's career. Declining in recent years to work on commission—he will make only what he wants to make, often spending hours on the kind of finish work that other artists delegate to studio assistants—Garry has kept many of his own early pieces around the house and

At rear in entrance hall LEFT is Bennett's "Noguchi on Sticks" bench; Honduras rosewood, mahogany, and dyed walnut, 1982. Tommy Simpson's "Boxer's Chair" DETAILS ABOVE AND OPPOSITE was made especially for Bennett in 1987. Materials are maple, mahogany, walnut, cherry, bits of ivory, leather, rope, and a boxer's pail, sponge, and towel embroidered with the name "Fireball Bennett" to commemorate the artists' shared enthusiasm for pugilism.

CONFIDENCE COURAGE

TENACITY

KEEP COOL

has also made special furnishings such as a stereo cabinet, kitchen cabinets, and a case to hold antique dolls. In 1974, when the Bennetts decided to expand the house to accommodate three children, now grown, and a large dog, Garry built one entire room, panel by panel, in his studio across the estuary in Oakland, casting the pewter brackets at a forge in Berkeley.

This exquisitely crafted environment is an ideal setting for the work of Garry's close friends and colleagues, who, like Bennett, are regarded as the best of the contemporary furniture makers: Wendell Castle, Judy Kensley McKie, Arthur Espenet Carpenter, Wendy Maruyama, Norman Petersen, and Tommy Simpson. The bringing together of some of their finest pieces in one place is a dazzling tribute to the creativity of an era and, particularly, to those West Coast furniture makers whose work is less often seen in East Coast collections. It is also a delightful way to live.

"We've only begun to purchase pieces in the last few years," explains Sylvia. "Eventually, I would like to replace every factory-produced piece of furniture we have with something handmade—but slowly, one piece at a time. When Garry sells a piece, then we can buy a piece." Sylvia's unhurried timetable for building the Bennett collection is perfectly compatible with her husband's approach to furniture making.

Garry, who spends seven days a week in his Oakland studio, does not work from drawings or plans, relying instead on spontaneous whims and free associations

OPPOSITE TOP Dining room viewed from living room, with Bennett's 1975 "Cabinet with Lights" at left. Cabinet is redwood with gold- and silver-plated copper and brass. At threshold is another of Bennett's benches DETAIL OPPOSITE BELOW, this one made in 1987 of dyed walnut and dousee with polychromed pigskin by K. Lee Manuel. Dining table, also by Bennett, has gold-plated cast-bronze feet, polychromed maple legs, and a lacquered maple top, 1988. Tall cabinet is by Judy Kensley McKie, milk-painted maple, 1984. Bennett's controversial "Nail" cabinet in padouk and glass, 1982, is visible in left-hand corner of dining room.

BELOW Another view of Bennett's "Cabinet with Lights," with Wendell Castle's "Three-Columned Table" in foreground. Made in one day while Castle was visiting Bennett, table has California walnut top supported by painted wood base, 1988. Visible in dining room beyond is Bennett's tilt-top table DETAIL RIGHT with removable lamp, 1980; cherry and ash with rotary-brushed aluminum, blued steel, and glass.

LEFT TO RIGHT Wendy Maruyama's "Mickey Mackintosh" chair, painted wood, one of a series made since 1986; one of Bennett's first furniture pieces, a Tonsu-inspired chest of drawers in pine, 1976, in front of which sits Arthur Espenet Carpenter's "Wishbone" chair in cherry with woven leather strap seat, 1980; closer view of Judy Kensley McKie's tall cabinet and Bennett's table (snake plate is also by McKie, as is turtle plate on top of Tonsu chest); and four-drawer chest-on-stand that resided at Blair House during Mondale vice-presidency, made by Bennett in 1976 of Douglas fir and lacewood, with etched and blued galvanized steel and handmade pulls DETAIL OVERLEAF.

to inspire his distinctive, sometimes eccentric furniture. He once described the process as follows:

I start out with something—a shape I want—in my head. Then I go around the shop and get pieces of wood and sometimes I'll stack them up and look at them. Mostly I just start sawing. I draw right on the board. Sometimes I paint it white so I can see it better. Then I draw with a pencil and do a lot of erasing. When I get the shape I want, I go for it.

The way in which the Bennetts live with their collection is just as spontaneous as the manner in which Garry designs and fabricates his own one-of-a-kind pieces. The table on which they dine was made by Garry; the tall cabinet that stores their

china is by Judy Kensley McKie ("I think it's just about the best piece of furniture I've ever seen"). In the living room, one turns on the overhead light that Garry fashioned before he took up furniture making, settles into Norman Petersen's chair, and puts down a drink on Judy Kensley McKie's glass-topped "Chase" table. There's Tommy Simpson's "Boxer's Chair" (made especially for Garry) in a corner near the front hall, where one of Garry's benches provides a convenient spot to pull on boots. A small chest of drawers (made by Garry) that sat in Blair House while Fritz Mondale was vice-president now holds family odd and ends. The deliberately disturbing "Nail" cabinet—a fine example of traditional cabinetmaking, which upon

closer inspection, reveals a raw nail imbedded in the otherwise perfect finish (Garry built the piece to prove he could do it, then pounded in the nail to show his irreverence for the accomplishment)—displays some of the Bennetts' antique and contemporary handmade bowls.

The ambivalence of the "Nail" cabinet also reveals something of Bennett's attitude toward the "art-versus-craft" debate in which so many critics of contemporary furniture making are embroiled. But whether, ultimately, Bennett himself is judged artist or craftsman—or, as is likely, both—one thing is certain: He and Sylvia have assembled one of the wittiest, most energetic, and discerning collections of handmade furniture in America today.

That Bennett is an artist obsessed with his craft can be seen at both the smaller scale of the Mondale cabinet DETAIL OPPOSITE and at the larger scale of the room he made, panel by panel, in 1974 DETAIL BELOW. Window mullions and frames are black dyed virgin redwood and redwood salvaged from old wine vats; pewter brackets were cast by Bennett himself at forge in Berkeley. Within room is low table of Douglas fir stained blue with stainless-steel trim, 1974, one of Bennett's earliest pieces.

Redwood bench behind it is another early Bennett piece, 1974. At left in room is Norman Petersen's steel and granite chair, 1987. "Cloud" floor lamp at right is by Bennett; aluminum and plastic, 1974.

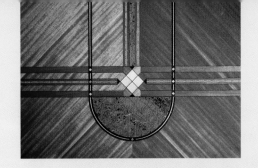

THE ARCHITECTURAL CONNECTION

When architects and craft artists collaborate, the results can be spectacular. Each brings to the work of the other an added dimension that makes the whole greater than the sum of its parts. Well-designed spaces take on a warmth and personality that even the best commercial finishes and furnishings seldom achieve. The discipline of architectural commissions pushes craft artists to explore new materials, new methods of fabrication, new ways of communicating their artistic visions. Large building projects provide opportunities for craft artists to work at a monumental scale, and they, in turn, bring to these projects a special liveliness—a sense of animation and the presence of a human spirit. At their most successful, these collaborations produce a unity, an organic wholeness that for more than a hundred years has been the Arts and Crafts ideal.

MONY HEADQUARTERS

When MONY Financial Services (formerly Mutual of New York) decided, like most of its competitors, to move back-office functions to the suburbs, then-chairman James Attwood hired architects Richard Kronick, Miguel Valcarcel, and Ruxandra Panaitescu to create a new image for the corporate staff headquarters slated to remain in the company's familiar Broadway building. Built in 1950 to plans drawn by Shreve, Lamb, and Harmon (architects of the Empire State Building) just before the outbreak of World War II, the building had a vaguely late-Deco quality, much diminished by renovations over time. In an effort to revive that quality and, at the same time, respond to Attwood's keen interest in woodworking, Kronick et al. engaged three furniture artists to work with them in developing an aesthetic reminiscent of the Deco-related Cranbrook style (page 19).

Using a combination of anigre and sycamore with ebony inlays for the architectural woodwork of the twelfth-floor corporate-communications center, the designers crafted a light, airy environment into which contemporary handmade furniture by Wendy Stayman, Bruce Volz, and

Redesigned lobby of MONY Financial Services world headquarters building OPPOSITE features custom-designed mahogany concierge desk and marble inlaid floor in diamond pattern that is picked up in border of custom carpet for twelfth-floor reception room. Hall table, by Peter Spadone, is curly maple and ebony, 1988; small side table, by Wendy Stayman, is curly maple and figured black bean inlaid with ebony, 1988; low coffee table, by Bruce Volz, is curly maple and ebony with a hand-rubbed lacquer finish, 1987. Floor lamp is Eliel Saarinen's brass, copper, and bronze torchiere, designed in 1929, specially remanufactured by Cranbrook Academy of Art for MONY project.

LEFT TO RIGHT Dining corridor with ceiling fixtures in diamond motif derived from lobby floor, bench by Wendy Stayman (cherry, curly maple, and ebony with black lacquered detail, 1988) and Eliel Saarinen's round table (1929–30) in the distance; private dining room with contract table and chairs, and smaller-scale version of monumental lobby chandelier; Wendy Stayman's side table mediates between Eliel Saarinen's chair (1929–30) and patterning of custom woodwork DETAIL FAR RIGHT.

Fabrics and furnishings were selected by designers Teri Figliuzzi and Catharine Tarver.

Peter Spadone fits as easily as though it were part of the architecture itself. Additional contract furnishings, which were carefully chosen to complement the three artists' work, and Eliel Saarinen's classic side chair complete the setting, which is, in a sense, a selective chronicle of mid-to-late-twentieth-century American woodworking. Moreover, since completion of the twelfth floor in 1988, MONY president Richard Farley has expanded the company's craft-furniture collection by commissioning artists Timothy Philbrick, James Schriber, and Ron Puckett to design additional pieces for his own office.

What is it that inspired James Attwood to take his company in such a noncorporate design direction, eschewing modern glass-and-steel as well as the traditional reproduction furniture found in executive offices coast to coast? "When I was growing up," he reminisced, "we had a number of Alvar Aalto pieces in our home—part of our Finnish heritage, I guess. Then, when I

had a chance to furnish my own office, I chose all Aalto pieces: chairs, low tables, rolling cart, even the bookshelves. Living with these things every day, I learned to love wood, the way in which it is crafted, the curves, the layers of lamination."

At the beginning of the recent renovation, Attwood was faced with something of a dilemma: While his own preference was for very light woods such as ash (much used by Aalto), his top executives strongly preferred darker woods such as walnut, which they associated with the trappings of financial stability. The architects' solution—a mid-range of honey-toned woods executed in panels and moldings that are classic rather than traditional—was particularly pleasing to Attwood because it evoked, for him, the interiors of Frank Lloyd Wright. "I found the whole process fascinating: The way the woods, fabrics, furniture, and lighting came together reminded me a little of the Arts and Crafts movement." According to Attwood, many others in the company share his enthusiasm. "Since we've moved into the new space, people are even starting to dress better—there's a sort of automatic dress code that goes with this furniture."

Attwood, who died last year, had only one reservation. "You know," he once mused, "I'm not sure what Aalto himself would think of all this. He designed his pieces for socialist institutions. Do you think he would approve of the way capitalism is putting his inspiration to work?"

THE RAINBOW ROOM

●

"We didn't want everything to be about nostalgia," insists Hugh Hardy of Hardy Holzman Pfeiffer Associates, the architects in charge of refurbishing two floors—including the fabled Rainbow Room—atop Rockefeller Center in New York City. So, with designer Milton Glaser, who created all new tableware and graphics for the project, Hardy brought in three glass artists to add a luster of contemporaneity to the imaginatively (as opposed to literally) restored spaces. Working with a committee that included representatives of major museums, the architects first identified locations that they felt were appropriate for the introduction of new pieces; then the committee members chose craft artists whom they believed were most appropriate for specific commissions.

For the elevated wall behind the bandstand of the Rainbow Room, Dan Dailey designed and fabricated a cast-glass composition called "Orbit," a sweeping depiction of planets hurtling through the universe. For the Buffet Pavilion, located on the opposite side of the floor, Dale Chihuly created a luminous frieze of hand-blown colored glass vessels shaped like

Refurbished Rainbow Room features contemporary craft artist Dan Dailey's cast glass "Orbit" wall DETAIL OPPOSITE.

Ray King's "Saturn" light, which recalls the theme of Dailey's "Orbit" wall, illuminates Rainbow Room foyer. Materials are patinated brass, crystal lenses, and etched optical-glass ring, with polished black granite base. OPPOSITE Dale Chihuly's handblown colored-glass vessels form a luminous frieze in the Buffet Pavilion. BELOW Dailey's Gumby-like sconces, with pair at left designating which restroom is which.

giant seashells. Throughout the lobbies are Ray King's "Saturn" table lights, while Dan Dailey's sconces—Gumby-like figures that dance in pairs along the walls—illuminate circulation spaces.

The imagery in all three artists' work is consistent with the themes—sea, cosmos, etc.—present in much of the original Rockefeller Center artwork; and, in the designs of Dailey and King, the spirit of Art Deco is very much alive. Yet all of these pieces are undeniably contemporary. There is no attempt to mimic the time or style in which Rockefeller Center was built, no use of craft as merely a restorationist's tool to recreate the past.

For Hardy Holzman Pfeiffer, the collaboration of architecture and craft is a familiar, almost routine process, not something invented for the Rainbow Room refurbishing. "We believe in collaboration, fundamentally," says Hardy. "It's how we do what we do. It's part of our cultural bias, our way of responding to what is going on in the other arts."

According to Hardy, the firm developed this bias in its struggle to humanize the

large-scaled institutional spaces that are the core of its practice. "How does one populate space without people?" Hardy asks. The answer in recent projects such as the Eugene (Oregon) Performing Arts Center, the Virginia Museum of Fine Arts, and the Anchorage (Alaska) Performing Arts Center (pages 148 to 149) has been to collaborate with glassmaker Ed Carpenter, metalworker Albert Paley, and other craft artists whose contributions appear every-

where from boldly patterned lobby carpeting to finely stenciled toilet doors.

By and large, the work of these craft artists is allowed to stand on its own and is not, as in so many collaborations, rigorously subordinated to the architecture. "We try to achieve a balance in our collaborations," explains Hardy. "For some things, we're very specific about what we want from an artist, and in other areas, we just say, 'Be my guest.' "

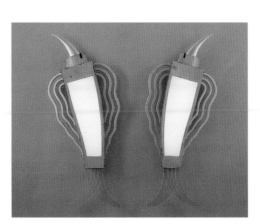

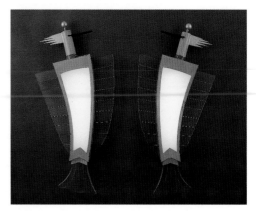

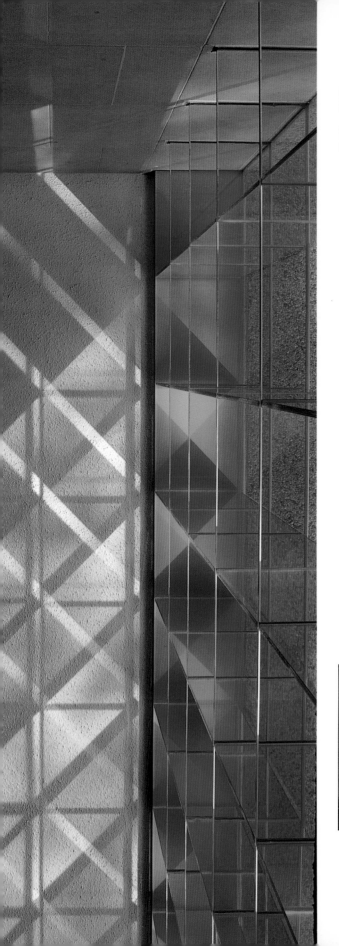

CHRISTIAN THEOLOGICAL SEMINARY

Chapel of architect Edward Larabee Barnes's Christian Theological Seminary in Indianapolis, illuminated by James Carpenter's innovative window of dichroic glass, a material familiar to most people as the filters used in color photography. Microthin layers of metallic oxide on glass selectively reflect and transmit specific wavelengths within the spectrum of light.

When architect Edward Larabee Barnes approached glass artist/technologist James Carpenter to design the windows for the chapel of his Christian Theological Seminary buildings in Indianapolis, it was with the express intention of avoiding the sentimentality or narrative quality so often found in religious windows, particularly stained glass. Instead, Barnes wanted his windows to deal exclusively with light, a challenge for which Carpenter—arguably the most technically advanced glassmaker in the United States—was well prepared by earlier work for the Hong Kong Bank.

After considering prisms for Barnes's chapel (a solution that proved too expensive), Carpenter developed an "egg-crate" grid of vertical clear glass stiffeners fitted with horizontal bands of dichroic glass that transmit light in varying colors and patterns as the angle and intensity of sunlight change. These patterns, enriched in experience by the movement and color of leaves reflected from trees just outside the windows, impart to the chapel a spiritual quality that exceeds, in its subtlety and complexity, both Barnes's and Carpenter's highest expectations.

ALASKA PERFORMING ARTS CENTER

The small subarctic city of Anchorage, with a population just over a quarter million and no architectural heritage to speak of, hardly seems an ideal location for a successful building commission. Yet architects Hardy Holzman Pfeiffer Associates have managed to accomplish just that, designing a complex of three stage houses (one a recycled landmark theater) that, together with their lobbies, support spaces, and multilevel connecting foyers, serve as the performing arts center for the entire state.

Part of the architects' challenge was to dispel the gloom of the northern winter during which the sun rises late and sets early, bringing little warmth to the frozen collection of recently constructed mid-rise office buildings, hotels, shopping streets, and two-story residential condominiums that is downtown Anchorage. The other part was budget: Limited from the outset, it was severely cut when Alaska's oil royalties—the source of funding for the Center —were suddenly diminished.

With expensive building materials and luxurious finishes out of the question, the architects turned to more creative solutions, introducing artists and craftspeople into the project. One of these was Oregon glassmaker Ed Carpenter (pages 174 to 177). For the curtain walls of the Center's lobby and corridor areas, Carpenter designed double-glazed panels in which are sealed mosaics of colored marbles and copper sheeting cut into tartan patterns. These panels bring warmth and life to the public spaces—a year-round reminder of the Alaskan summer, when days are long and bright and the world is, briefly, some color other than white.

ABOVE Four of the twenty-six "Labyrinth" mosaic panels designed by glassmaker Ed Carpenter for the Alaska Performing Arts Center in Anchorage, 1988. Each panel is composed of colored marbles and patterned copper sheeting sealed in double glazing.

HOME BOX OFFICE

Reception area of HBO's headquarters BELOW establishes subdued Art Deco vocabulary that carries throughout fifteen floors of corporate offices, including private dining rooms BELOW RIGHT AND OPPOSITE. Dining table, designed by furniture maker Jack Larimore in collaboration with architect Anthony Tsirantonakis, is Honduras mahogany, curly maple, purpleheart, and lacewood with dyed wood inlays, 1984.

In 1984, having outgrown the headquarters of Time, Inc., its parent company, Home Box Office moved its rapidly expanding cable-TV business into a completely gutted and rehabed building on Sixth Avenue (known as "Network Row") at Forty-second Street, just on the fringe of New York's theater district. Because of the age and character of the original building—it was built in 1906, then expanded vertically in 1926—and given the "show biz" character of the company, architects Judy Swanson and Anthony Tsirantonakis developed what they term a "soft Deco" image for the new HBO interiors. Strong horizontal banding and decorative wall sconces carry throughout fifteen floors of general office, executive, food-service, and entertainment spaces, with functions being differentiated primarily by changing colors, materials, and detailing.

When the time came to select furnishings for the boardroom and the private dining complex, the architects were hard-

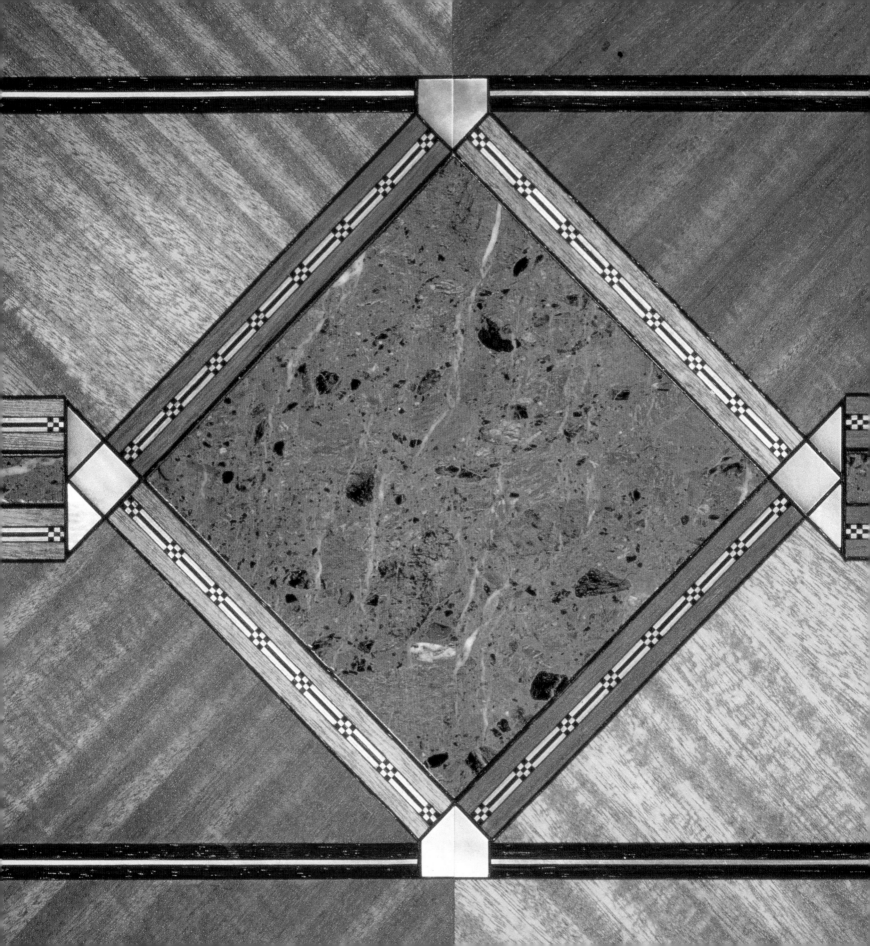

pressed to find contract tables compatible with the character of the space and still within the client's budget. So they recommended that HBO hire furniture artists to work with the design team in a collaborative relationship that was, at the time, almost unheard of in the world of corporate-facilities management. Skeptical at first (how does one control costs? guarantee delivery?), HBO agreed: Show business is, after all, fraught with creative risk taking.

Happily, the first proposal came in under the allocated budget. Having reviewed slides of dozens of furniture artists catalogued by The Gallery at Workbench, Tsirantonakis selected woodworker Rick Wrigley to design and build the boardroom table. Working together, the two developed drawings and models exploring different ways in which the table could become part of the room itself. A preferred direction was priced, then developed in detail by Wrigley, built in his shop, and completed—before the boardroom itself was finished and for less money than a customized-contract or commercial-millwork table would have cost.

At the same time, Tsirantonakis was working with Philadelphia furniture maker Jack Larimore (pages 244 to 245) on the private dining room tables, which, while distinctly different from Wrigley's piece, have a similar inlaid character and awareness of Tsirantonakis's architecture. These tables have been so successful that, three years after move-in, HBO commissioned Larimore to make additional pieces for the headquarters. "We had our doubts, at first," admits a company spokesperson, "but everyone loves these tables. They're beautiful, they've held up well, and working with these craft artists has been a tremendous pleasure. I'm very glad we did it."

Architectural detailing of HBO's boardroom is picked up in furniture maker Rick Wrigley's table, designed in collaboration with Tsirantonakis and executed in wenge and mahogany with inlays of sterling silver, mother-of-pearl, and verde antique marble, 1984.

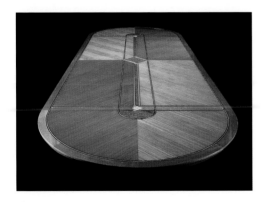

PANDICK PRESS OFFICES

English brown oak veneer is predominant in architectural finishes and in Wrigley's conference table/desk BELOW and reception desk RIGHT AND OPPOSITE. Wrigley's furniture also incorporates white oak solids, acacia burl, and anigre veneers with inlays of ebony and holly. Rosewood and holly checkered banding at base of reception desk is picked up in piping on Josef Hoffman's "Villa Gallia" armchairs OPPOSITE.

When an architect wants to integrate furniture with interior finishes, the usual solution is to design both and give the furniture drawings to a custom millwork shop, where the less apparent details and means of construction are worked out by an anonymous craftsman. Not so in the case of Pandick, Inc.'s executive offices, where architects Randolph Gerner and Anne Manning engaged woodworker Rick Wrigley to design and make the "signature" furnishings (reception desk, boardroom table, and president's conference table/desk) in close collaboration with the development of Manning's architectural concept.

In a manner reminiscent of the American Arts and Crafts movement, Manning applied English brown oak to all the door

*Rick Wrigley's table for the Pandick boardroom
is English brown oak veneer with white oak
solids, acacia burl, and anigre with inlays of
verde antique marble, mother-of-pearl, ebony,
and holly. Doors leading to boardroom and
manager's office OPPOSITE BELOW show
more complex geometric patterning developed
with mullioned glass.*

frames, wall panels, baseboards, chair rails, cornice moldings, and closet doors in a simple geometric patterning. When applied to the more important architectural features of the space, such as the screen walls and mullioned glass doors, the patterning becomes significantly richer and more complex.

The same patterning is picked up in Wrigley's furniture pieces, which, like the architectural finishes, are enhanced with minimal inlays of verde antique marble as well as exotic woods and mother-of-pearl. To supplement Wrigley's furniture, Manning chose the "Villa Gallia" armchair (designed in 1913 by architect Josef Hoffmann of the Wiener Werkstätte), a classic modern piece that reinforces the Arts and Crafts spirit of the Pandick space. Even the piping on the chair—a fairly subtle detail—is consciously related to the rosewood and holly banding at the base of the reception desk.

The result is so unified, aesthetically, that it is impossible to say whether the interior finishes have inspired the furniture, or vice versa. Yet the furniture has a strength and character that clearly sets it apart from ordinary millwork. Wrigley's pieces are not just objects wrapped in the same veneers as the space around them: Each stands on its own; each has an integrity that comes from the inherent logic of furniture making—as opposed to the mere "skinning" of volumetric forms that typifies most architects' efforts to coordinate custom-designed furniture with wall, floor, and/or ceiling finishes.

THE ARTIST'S VISION

■

Today's craft artists are a new breed working in an age-old tradition. Well educated in the fine and liberal arts, most of them have received formal training in graduate programs where they've studied and apprenticed with master craftsmen of the immediate postwar era. They know one another well and, together with their galleries and their most supportive patrons, form a tight network that is concentrated primarily in New England, upstate New York, southeastern Pennsylvania, and the San Francisco Bay Area. Aware that they are part of a movement, they nonetheless shun identification with any common agenda; there are no prevailing schools of thought, no stylistic trends to which today's craft artists subscribe. Their work is highly individualistic, intensely personal, and constantly evolving. And because they are relatively young, it is likely that the best of their work is yet to come.

GLASS

RAY KING

■ Ray King is not just a glassmaker. He is a "maker of places" who uses glass as his principal material. His studio is filled with formed metal, sophisticated lighting devices, intricate scale models, and life-size cardboard mock-ups used to design the large mixed media installations that are the mainstay of his business.

"People who like craft-gallery glass do not collect me," says King, and that is understandable. King is by nature a builder, a nuts-and-bolts artisan who is fascinated with engineering and the details of construction. Most of what he produces is architectural in conception, if not in actual application.

For example, his light fixtures: While some are exhibited in galleries as individual art objects, these powerful pieces are most effective in collaborative installations such as the refurbished Rainbow Room in New York City's Rockefeller Center (pages 142 to 145). That commission was particularly successful because King's fascination

Cosmopolitan Apartment sconces are composed of half-inch laminated glass sheets OPPOSITE cut into saw-toothed fins, which King places with strips of gasketing between bronze forms and bolts into place.

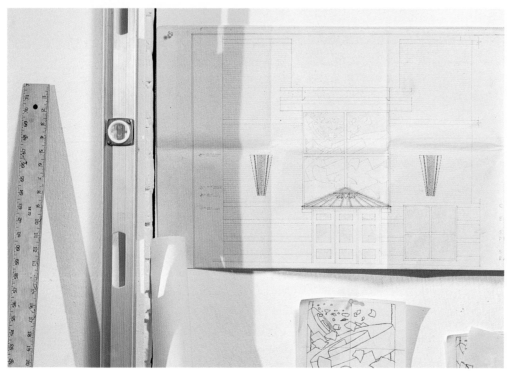

with radial and energized lines so closely corresponds to the Art Deco sensibility that designer Milton Glaser and architect Hugh Hardy were seeking to restore to the famous 1930s ballroom and restaurant complex when they undertook renovation of the top two floors of Rockefeller Center in 1988.

"I am interested in layers," says King, "layers of form, lighting, structure." In the late 1970s, he began a series of leaded clear and colored glass screens inspired by "formlings," which, according to King, is the name given by anthropologists to ghostlike shapes that float over realistic figures in prehistoric cave paintings found in Southern Rhodesia. It is from images of these "formlings" that the "drifting sheet" motif in King's work has evolved. "My early 'formlings' have shadows that are intensely colored, as though an alien light were projecting through them and onto a surface beneath. It is the feeling of movement, of floating that I was after."

Although King is currently experimenting with lighting as a means of translating the feeling of movement into movement itself, the "formlings" are still very much present in his work. For example, in his

King's studio is a nineteenth-century chocolate warehouse in downtown Philadelphia, where two or three assistants work on metal drill presses and glass-cutting machines while King assembles finished components. Some of these, such as frame for canopy of the Cosmopolitan Apartments (model and drawings, OPPOSITE), are so large that they have to be welded in adjoining alley and lifted out with a crane.

window for Philadelphia's venerable S. S. White Building, recently rehabilitated and expanded into the Cosmopolitan Apartments, they are carved into clear glass (which gives them a less surreal, more abstract quality than those depicted in the earlier colored and leaded screens) and combined with a spiral in what King calls an "infinity drawing": a cosmic composition arbitrarily trimmed at the lines of the window frame. The spiral is another form that King has been developing in his work, inspired by a dramatic sighting of the aurora borealis in Alaska that confirmed his intuition. "It was all there," King recounts, "light, color, movement, and a perfect spi-

ral—exactly what I had been trying for all those years to achieve."

To carve this pattern into the one-half/three-quarter-inch laminated window, King first masks the glass with a stenciling material made for etching tombstones, then takes it into a sandblasting chamber, where it is etched with an aluminum-oxide grit applied under high pressure. For etching the glass fins of huge sconces that flank the Cosmopolitan window, the process is similar, except that no masking is required. When installed, these sconces will be fitted with metal halide HID fixtures that throw light both up and down, as well as illuminate the etched glass fins with a soft glow.

Radial sections of King's bronze and glass sconces for Cosmopolitan Apartments are clamped together prior to marking, punching, and cutting of holes that will be fitted with clear glass hemispheres. Much of punching and cutting is done by assistants using machines such as water-cooled glass cutter RIGHT that King himself has adapted from more conventional woodworking equipment.

Similarly, special lighting installed underneath the radial point of a glass canopy cantilevered over the Cosmopolitan doors will not only illuminate the entrance but will transmit light to the cut-glass edge at the outer perimeter. Indeed, it is all there: structure, form, light, movement—the synergy for which King is striving.

King, who began as an apprentice to a Philadelphia stained glassmaker in 1970, is today one of the best-known architectural glassmakers in the United States—perhaps, in the world. Although his Philadelphia location and the site-specific nature of his work tend to concentrate his commissions in the southeastern Pennsylvania region, he is collected and exhibited by institutions as far away as the Victoria and Albert Museum and the Royal Institute of British Architects in London; the Sanske Galerie in Zurich; Hulturhuset in Stockholm; and the Hokkaido Museum of Modern Art in Sapporo, Japan. King's work can regularly be seen in the Corning Museum of Glass and in the American Craft Museum, and he has also completed commissions in such far-flung locations as Atlanta, Georgia, and Fairbanks, Alaska.

His wife, Marsha Hall, a free-lance writer, handles the studio's paperwork, while their young son, Julian, plays with his dad's architectural models. Those models are central to King's mission in the world of glassmaking: "What I want most is to dispel from craft the connotation of 'the little gallery on Main Street.' That's not what my work is about. Craft, for me, is part of the process of making spaces."

SUSAN STINSMUEHLEN-AMEND

■ An artist who uses glass as a medium of rebellion against conventional notions of beauty and decorum, Susan Stinsmuehlen-Amend brings a level of energy and inventiveness to her work that is conspicuously missing from much handmade architectural glass. From 1973 to 1987, when she moved to Hollywood, California, she was a partner in the Renaissance Glass Company, Austin, Texas, a business that provided her with enough economic stability to allow exploration of the more creative, less traditional qualities of glass. This exploration, in turn imparts to her commercial glass the originality characteristic of her art pieces.

"Perhaps the greatest value of her production," according to fellow glassmaker Narcissus Quagliata (page 93), "... has been her capacity to enlarge her audience's perception of what is feasible in glass by bringing [to it] ideas most often dealt with in the larger world of painters, sculptors, video artists, et al." Stinsmuehlen-Amend's influence over other glassmakers is attributable as much to her lectures, workshops, and conferences as it

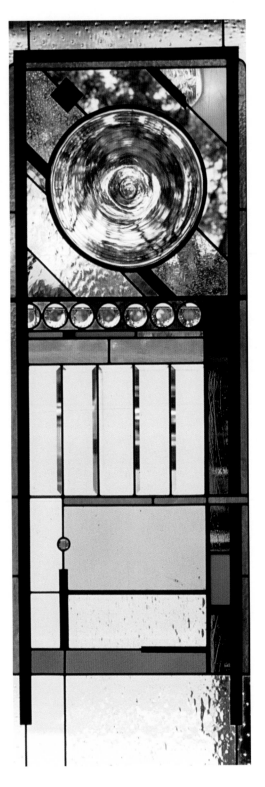

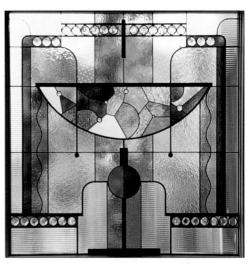

Susan Stinsmuehlen-Amend's architectural glasswork, though more conventional than her independent art pieces, brings innovation and surprise to the medium. LEFT TO RIGHT "Arched Post" door panel, 1985; "Diagonal with Del" leaded glass door with hand-blown roundel used in feature film D.O.A., 1986-1987; double doors and panel for bathroom, both designed for a private residence in 1985.

is to the critical acclaim that her work has been accorded over the last ten years.

Graduated in fine arts from the University of Texas at Austin after attending Hood College and Indiana University, she has taught workshops at the famous Pilchuck Glass Center in Washington and has served as both a board member and president of the Glass Art Society. A frequent guest artist, she has lectured everywhere from the Rhode Island School of Design to the Japanese Glass Conference in Tsumagoi and the Ausglass Conference in Melbourne. By demystifying glass and challenging traditional ideas about how it ought to look, Stinsmuehlen-Amend brings new life to this ancient craft.

MARNI BAKST

The freshness and spontaneity of Marni Bakst's stained glass is unusual in a medium that, because of the many steps involved in fabrication, can reduce an artist's original sketch concepts to designs that are, graphically, rather static. Using lead not only to delineate shapes and impart structural integrity, she also appliques it in irregular patterns that override the cut edges of the glass pieces, giving to her compositions a characteristic delicacy and sweeping movement.

Bakst, who was graduated from the California College of Arts and Crafts in Oakland and apprenticed at the Greenland Studio in New York City, now has her studio in Los Angeles. In addition to numerous residential commissions, she has designed the "Rainbow Wall" for Marble Collegiate Church, windows for the Chapel of St. Frances Cabrini, and a major installation for the Cooper Square Site I Housing Development —all located on New York City's Manhattan Island.

Artificially lighted wall DETAIL OPPOSITE for La Delice, a restaurant in Whippany, New Jersey.

LEFT TO RIGHT *Stairwell window, installed by Bakst in a Connecticut residence, 1982; sliding pocket doors of Pat and Judy Coady's former Brooklyn residence; detail of Coady doors showing reused fragment of original nineteenth-century glass; and bedroom window for a New Jersey residence, 1980.*

ELLEN MANDELBAUM

Ellen Mandelbaum, an award-winning New York City stained-glass artist, works primarily with architects (such as Brian Perceval, Wasserman & Waterhouse, and Adina Taylor) because she believes that conditions of context and client requirements tend to enrich rather than constrain design. "Seeing the light and where the piece is in space—I like architectural glass because of these elements."

A graduate of the Horschule fur Bildenck Kunste, Berlin, and from Indiana University with both a B.A. and an M.F.A. in painting, Mandelbaum began studying glassmaking at The Stained Glass School in North Adams, Massachusetts, in 1975. The process by which she makes her delicate, evocative pieces is essentially the same as that used since the twelfth century.

First, a full-size drawing, or cartoon, of the overall design is made, complete with lead lines. This is traced onto brown paper much like a dressmaker's pattern, then each individual piece is cut out with a special scissors that allows for the thickness of the lead lines. Pattern pieces are laid on selected colors and types of glass, and a glass cutter is used to score around them. Pressure along the score lines breaks the pieces out; the artist then arranges them in the desired pattern and wraps them with lead strips. Mandelbaum also paints on her compositions, using metal-oxide powders bound by gum arabic and fired in a kiln. This technique, which adds a soft, organic quality to her abstract, geometric designs, fascinates Mandelbaum. "There are various densities up to a point and then you can scratch through; that's the most exciting part of all."

BELOW A portion of leaded-glass picture window that Ellen Mandelbaum designed and made for a private residence in 1986. OPPOSITE Detail of leaded and hand-painted glass panel for summer porch. Named the "Roberta Window," it was completed in 1984.

ED CARPENTER

West Coast glassmaker Ed Carpenter works out of Portland, Oregon, where he has been producing architectural commissions since 1972. Beginning with residential installations, his focus has shifted gradually over the years to large-scale public buildings and corporate and religious commissions, for which he designs monumental windows, skylights, screens, and lighting fixtures. The stepson of Robert Alexander (a partner during the 1950s with famed modern architect Richard Neutra), Carpenter spent many summers accompanying the family on architectural pilgrimages and working as an office boy in his stepfather's firm.

After attending the University of California at Santa Barbara and at Berkeley, Carpenter spent the better part of four years abroad, visiting glass factories, window installations, and glass artists throughout Europe. During these periods, he studied

Detail of interior glass screen for Mark Saw Chain headquarters, Milwaukie, Oregon, designed by Ed Carpenter in collaboration with Griggs Lee Rutt Architects, 1981. Screen is constructed of leaded, etched, and sandblasted glass, both handblown and machine-made.

*Atrium window of Kaiser Permanente Medical
Center in Portland, Oregon, was designed by
Carpenter in collaboration with Broom,
Oringdulph, O'Toole and Rudolph, Architects.
Completed in 1985, it was, like all of
Carpenter's larger installations, fabricated by
master glass craftsman Tim O'Neil. Skylight of
The Aberdeen OPPOSITE TOP, a nine-story
office building in Dallas, Texas, is composed of
650 colored and clear scientific prisms that,
through use of mirrors, reflect rays of sun
throughout 350-foot concourse. Designed in
collaboration with architects Taylor-Hewlett,
skylight was installed 1986. BELOW LEFT
Skylight for private residence; mirrors, prisms,
and hand-blown glass, 1989.*

*BELOW RIGHT Foyer window of the
Portland, Oregon, Justice Center, designed in
collaboration with architects Zimmer Gunsul
Frasca and completed 1983. Composed of
mirror glass in strips (beveled to cast rainbows
on interior surfaces) and equilateral triangles
heat-fused to squares of beveled plate glass, the
window is a combined diagonal and orthogonal
grid that interacts with geometry of supporting
framework. Conventional leading, cut glass,
and handblown glass from France, Germany,
and Seattle are also incorporated into
Carpenter's pattern, which is designed as a
scintillating abstraction of ever-changing light
and color.*

stained-glass design and technique in Buckinghamshire, England, with Patrick Reyntiens (collaborator with John Piper at Liverpool Cathedral), and large architectural stained-glass design in Alsdorf, West Germany, with master glassmaker Ludwig Schaffrath. A former member of the board of trustees of the renowned Oregon School of Arts and Crafts, Carpenter continues to serve as a board member of the American Craft Council and was, from 1983 to 1986, chairman of the board of American Craft Enterprises.

Among the many architects with whom Carpenter has collaborated over the last fifteen years are such major firms as Hardy Holzman Pfeiffer Associates of New York City and Zimmer Gunsul Frasca of Port-

land, Oregon. What he looks for in the work of a prospective collaborator is "a sense of hierarchy [that results in] some areas wanting more detail than others. . . . The key is that the buildings have small forms and large forms in some kind of progression," he explains. "At the smaller end of those forms, I can be of assistance."

CONSTANCE LESLIE

■ "I first came to clay as a medium for sculpture," explains Constance Leslie, who received her bachelor's degree in fine arts from the Rhode Island School of Design (RISD) in 1972. "It was the immediacy of the clay modeling process that I liked best about sculpting and, after a while, I realized that what I wanted to be was not a sculptor, but a ceramicist." Leslie, who never studied traditional ceramics or trained as a potter, is today one of the most accomplished makers of handcrafted ceramic architectural details in the United States. Although she continues to produce individual tiles—mostly with applied three-dimensional forms or figures that compose into larger elements such as friezes or murals—it is cornices, moldings, and columns that she is most interested in creating.

"I got fascinated with columns while I was traveling in Spain several years ago. The figural qualities and ornamentation of

Constance Leslie and daughter, Poole, in Leslie's Providence, Rhode Island, studio. In addition to architectural details for which she is best known, Leslie makes multicolored blocks, balls, pyramids, and cylinders as individual sculptural forms, shown OPPOSITE before firing and glazing.

On upper floor of old horse barn that is now her studio, Leslie draws while Poole naps. Glazing and firing are done on ground floor, where Leslie's kiln is located.

After clay is molded or hand-built into desired shape, it is bisque-fired, then painted with hand-mixed commercial glazes and quick-fired by the Japanese raku method. OPPOSITE TOP rolling pin used by Leslie's studio assistant, Beth Ozgrow, to roll out clay before it is cut and shaped. BOTTOM Leslie uses book on trout to find colors for glazing clay fish.

Romanesque columns are a natural point of departure for sculpture. Architects have always played around with Romanesque columns in a way that they've never felt free to do with the classical orders. In fact, I also love Corinthian capitals, and I'm now starting to play around with them, too."

While disclaiming any real knowledge of architectural history, Leslie admits that architecture has been an important part of her life. Both her mother (now retired) and brother are architects; many of her commissions came directly from architects rather than through a gallery; and one of her best clients, Laura Rose, is a designer.

Almost all of Leslie's skills are self-taught. For example, her unorthodox method of glazing and firing: Leslie molds her one-of-a-kind pieces in a basic white stone clay body ("I'm not interested in mixing my own clays or creating weird, unknown clay bodies"), bisque fires them, and then applies hand-mixed commercial glazes. After glazing, her pieces are quick-fired by the Japanese raku method to give them a different finish with more depth than that produced by either commercial or traditional raku glazes. Her method of presenting design ideas to clients—in watercolors—is also self-taught, and she does her own working drawings. "I paint and draw a lot because I love working with surfaces; even my early involvement with clay was two-dimensional."

Leslie's greatest satisfaction in her work comes from being able to "finish" a space: "It's important to pay attention to the details in a room, just as it's important to pay

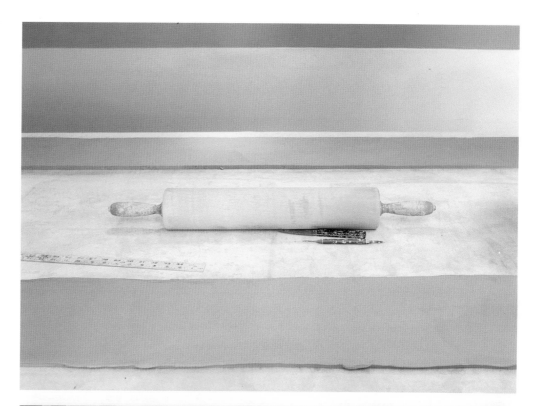

Sensuous form and exquisitely subtle color are hallmarks of Leslie's work, as in fireplace ABOVE AND RIGHT created for home of Providence designer Laura Rose, 1987. Kitchen columns and frieze OPPOSITE were designed and installed for Rose in 1985.

attention to the details in life. I have a great respect for the artisans who once did this kind of work routinely." By "this kind of work," Leslie means craft, which she defines as "usually utilitarian or lived with, and made by hand." For her, the "cosmic leap into fine art" that characterizes much of what is going on in contemporary craft is not necessarily a good thing: "It tends to make what is being produced 'too good' to be part of the environment; suddenly it has to be kept under glass." Speaking of her own work, Leslie says, "There are days when I'm an artist and days when I'm truly not. In both instances, my hands may be in the clay, but I'm doing things in very different ways."

Married to Warren Barker, a Westport, Massachusetts, boat builder who often helps with the firing of her work, Leslie has her studio in an old horse barn adjacent to the Barkers' former house in Providence, Rhode Island. Westport to Providence is a one-hour trip that Leslie makes almost daily, accompanied by her infant daughter, Lydia Poole Barker. While Leslie and her assistant, Beth Ozgrow, are busy rolling out clay, hand-building pieces, or painting glazes, Poole naps in a quiet corner or is tended by a baby-sitter.

A recurring motif in Leslie's work are trout, which she makes in plaster-of-Paris molds created from real fish. "I'm a trout fisherman," says Leslie, "and I love making them because the gleam on their bodies is exactly what the raku process produces. Perhaps when I'm sixty, I'll stop working in clay and go fishing."

ELIZABETH MACDONALD

Elizabeth MacDonald makes columns, walls, and architecturally inspired panels out of hundreds of small multihued tiles (the largest are no more than three and one-half inches square) mounted on wood and masonite substructures so that the tones of adjacent squares blend to create "canvases": painterly landscapes, skies, seascapes, and abstract compositions suggestive of geological or archaeological striations. "I am intrigued with the layers of history and color," says MacDonald, "how each layer reveals something else." Her individual tiles, with their rough stuccolike texture and slightly rounded corners are, in themselves, somewhat geological or archaeological in quality, giving to her compositions a presence that is, at once earthy and ethereal.

MacDonald, who worked in professional theater for almost ten years, established her Bridgewater, Connecticut, pottery studio in 1970. Since then, she has been producing corporate and private commissions as well as exhibition work that has won numerous awards such as a coveted Gold Medal in the Faenza (Italy) International Competition.

Elizabeth MacDonald completed fireplace wall LEFT for Warren Rubin–Bernice Wollman's western Connecticut home in 1988. Tiles are stoneware painted with color slips pressed into powdered stains, then fired at 2,100 degrees Fahrenheit, and mounted on wood. The column-and-lintel door frame ABOVE is in MacDonald's Connecticut studio, 1985. OPPOSITE Detail from one of her many wall installations showing characteristic color, texture, and compositional technique of MacDonald's tile work.

BETTY WOODMAN

A ceramicist whose work is shown in prestigious New York City art galleries as often as it is seen in craft exhibitions, Betty Woodman began about ten years ago to work at an architectural scale, creating pilasters, attached columns, dadoes, door frames, and entire rooms out of pottery. Most of this is imaginary architecture, assembled for museum or gallery shows and then dispersed. Recently, however,

Woodman has undertaken commissions for permanent installations, such as the room she has just finished for Whitney Museum director Tom Armstrong in his home on Fishers Island.

Trained at the Alfred University School for American Craftsmen, from which she was graduated in 1950, Woodman has been exhibiting her work and teaching ceramics since the mid-1970s. For the last ten years, she has been Associate Professor in the Fine Arts Department at the University of Colorado (Boulder), maintaining studios in both New York City and Italy. Her vessels and architectural fragments are widely collected by museums both in the United States and abroad, including the Metropolitan Museum of Art in New York; the Victoria and Albert Museum in London; the International Ceramic Museum in Faenza, Italy; the Boston Museum of Fine Arts; and the Carnegie-Mellon Institute in Pittsburgh.

Ceramicist Betty Woodman's architectural elements occur mostly in interior spaces of galleries and museums, but her "Window with Flower Boxes" LEFT provides imaginary fenestration suggesting views to gardens and hills beyond. Details RIGHT AND OPPOSITE are from a 1988 gallery show.

ALBERT PALEY

According to Albert Paley, one of the most important factors in his becoming the preeminent metal artist-craftsman in the United States today has been luck. "My timing all along was right. If I had emerged as a large-scale metalworker in the 1950s or 1960s, the response to my work would not have been nearly so warm as it has been." It was in 1972, just when the Postmodern movement in architecture was creating a demand for the kind of ornament previously eschewed by Bauhaus and Scandinavian designers, that Paley received his first architectural commission: the now-famous portal gates at the Renwick Gallery in Washington, D.C. Prior to that, he had been making jewelry, having graduated in 1969 from Temple University's Tyler School of Art with an M.F.A. in goldsmithing. Prophetically, Paley's jewelry was as monumental in feeling as his early monumental work, such as the Renwick gates, was jewelrylike in its intricate design and highly precise construction.

Since 1972, Paley has received more than twenty other architectural commissions, won fifteen major awards and grants, been collected by twenty of the

Twisting of heated metal bars produces whiplash curves, spiraling forms, and spiky thrusts that many observers see as linking the work of Albert Paley (at center of photo) to Art Nouveau—a mistaken notion, according to critic Penelope Hunter-Stiebel, who points out that "Paley does not mirror plant contours or mimic their blossoms: The shapes of concern to Paley are those that the steel assumes by itself in reaction to the stimuli he provides."

RIGHT Paley, wearing his high school graduation tuxedo, stands beside forged and fabricated mild steel and slate plant stand made in 1984. BELOW Old studio where all forging is done. The rest of the processes occur in Paley's new studio, a two-story space in downtown Rochester, New York. ABOVE LEFT TO RIGHT Renwick Gallery gates, 1974, forged, fabricated, and mild steel inlaid with brass, bronze, and copper; state capital building gates in Albany, New York, 1980, forged and fabricated mild steel, brass, and bronze; and gates for Washington, D.C., Marriott Hotel, 1983, forged mild steel and brass.

most important art museums in the United States, and holds a chair in the College of Fine and Applied Arts at the Rochester Institute of Technology. Working out of a studio and forge in Rochester, New York, he now employs thirteen assistants, including an office manager to handle paperwork, so that he can undertake more than one project at a time—something he could not do in his first shop, where, for many years, he worked with only one assistant. That shop, located in a ramshackle shed on a factory parking lot, was converted to a forge (where all the dirty work still goes on) when, in 1985, he moved his finishing and assembly operations to a much larger, more elaborate space that has, in addition to running water (one of many amenities that the old studio lacked), an exhibition area, offices, and conference rooms.

These concessions to the world of business meetings, exhibition planning, and design reviews reflect Paley's integral relationship with the architectural process that underlies his large-scale work. "Architects have been my main support," Paley explains, "and I like to get involved with them at the very beginning of a project. I want my work to respond to the nature of space, to help shape it." To be an effective part of this collaborative process, Paley must keep in close touch with the outside world, even though frequent phone calls and visits are an interruption to the noisy, sooty, back-breaking work that he would prefer to spend all his hours doing.

Paley is seen by historians as a key figure in the revival of large-scale metal craft, which, by the 1950s in the United States and Great Britain, had declined to the

point where only a few blacksmiths, working in isolation and without formal design training, were mostly reproducing familiar, time-worn designs. Not only has Paley appealed to a much wider public than had heretofore commissioned wrought ironwork, but his highly original design is the first break with stylistic tradition since the Art Nouveau and Art Deco movements of the early twentieth century.

Paley's sometimes disturbing originality springs from an intense intellectuality that is as much a part of his art as is his skill and technical daring. Torturing mild steel (a low-carbon material that is purer than wrought iron but similar in appearance) to the limits of its endurance, he deliberately leaves tool imprints, incisions, tears, twists, and burns to "record the evolutionary nature of process and form development. . . .

What I am trying to do is find the extremes of the material, to understand the vocabulary, then to develop a design concept that can use it." In this, he sees himself opposed to the prevailing aesthetic contemporary art in which "*image* is all-pervasive and the material is no more than a vehicle for its manifestations. Sensibilities of material are integral to my form development."

Sometimes, the unpleasantness of a form will fascinate Paley as much as the elegance and refinement for which his work is known. Beauty, he believes, can be defined by ugliness, as in a cactus: "brutal, primitive, hostile but which creates delicate, ephemeral flowers whose preciousness is emphasized by contrast." Judged over time and in terms of the thinking behind it, its inventiveness, artistic quality, and technical mastery—as well as contribution to the built environment—Albert Paley's work may be the greatest achievement of the late-twentieth-century craft movement.

ABOVE Rendering of Paley's Central Park Zoo gates, 1983–1987. After Paley worked four years on this proposal, lack of funding brought project to a halt. Full size maquette OPPOSITE is evidence of New York City's loss.

GREG AND LYDIA LEAVITT

■ She designs and he forges. To-gether, the husband-and-wife team of Greg and Lydia Leavitt create gardens of delphiniums, poppies, lilies, columbines, and birds of paradise—all wrought in metal and sometimes painted with Rust-Oleum to produce a shock of naturalistic color on realistically formed blossoms.

Working out of Upper Bank Forge in Lenni, Pennsylvania, Greg uses a combi-nation of modern metal-fabricating tech-niques and the ancient art of blacksmithing (in which metal is heated to 1,900 degrees Fahrenheit in a coal or propane fire, then pulled out and banged into shape during the forty-five seconds before it has to be reheated) to shape mild steel, Cor-Ten steel, copper, and bronze into gates, fences, window grilles, and other architec-tural elements. A metalworker since 1972 (he switched from business administration early on), Greg apprenticed with Chris-topher Ray (following pages) as well as other noted masters. For both private and public installations, he works on an individual-commission basis, producing site-specific pieces found throughout the Philadelphia—Wilmington area.

Terrace railing LEFT was forged by Greg Leavitt in mild steel for Haverford, Pennsylvania, residence, 1987. Wife Lydia made ceramic "leaf-shell" that is luminous element of outdoor sconce forged by Greg in mild steel, 1987.

Details of the Leavitts' "Peacock" gate LEFT AND BELOW located in Gladwyn, Pennsylvania. Gate is forged mild steel, copper, and bronze, 1987. OPPOSITE Forged and polychromed mild steel "Delphinium" gate installed in wall of Upper Bank Nursery, Media, Pennsylvania, was featured at the Philadelphia Flower Show, 1986. Greg describes his and Lydia's work as "sculpture on hinges."

CHRISTOPHER RAY

After graduating from the Philadelphia Academy of Fine Arts in 1960, Christopher Ray was a wood sculptor for several years before turning to iron, a medium that he learned from Howard Keyser, a traditional Gothic-style master blacksmith whom Ray assisted in forging gates for Washington's National Cathedral. Since then, he has been making fountains, outdoor sculptures, and forged iron gates for private and corporate clients all across the United States. In addition to forging, Ray does computer-aided design for architectural ironwork and has recently expanded into frame structures found in landscape settings: pergolas, gazebos, and arbors. Often combining the mythical with the real in his designs, he uses plant and animal forms as universal symbols: "primal images that have been used by so many cultures over the course of history. It's like genetic memory."

Christopher Ray's forged iron "Wissahickon Valley" gate DETAIL LEFT incorporates thirteen creatures that represent the valley and its life. Installed in 1980 at Thirteenth and Chestnut streets in Philadelphia, it sits in deep masonry frame so that, when open, it acts as bas relief against wall.

RICHARD JOHNSTON

Richard Johnston's cocktail table RIGHT is one-half-inch steel with yellow lacquer finish and a three-quarter-inch glass top, 1988. His glass-topped dining table BELOW is one-quarter-inch mild steel, sandblasted, with a surface coat of clear lacquer, 1988.

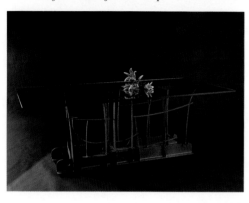

■ Known primarily in the Salt Lake City area, where he teaches three-dimensional design, sculpture, and computer graphics at the University of Utah, Richard Johnston is a metalworker/sculptor whose furniture, particularly, displays an unusual interest in form and volume. Working in a vocabulary derived more from industrial construction and modern sculpture than from the familiar Gothic, Baroque, or Art Nouveau traditions, Johnston produces pieces that are decidedly architectural rather than decorative in concept. Yet the sculptural qualities of his work are so dominant that his tables, fences, and other functional pieces tend to read as art objects first and as usable furnishings (which they are) only upon further investigation.

Johnston, a 1968 graduate of the Cranbrook Academy of Art with an M.F.A. in studio art, has completed about twenty major commissions and exhibited in some sixty-five museum and gallery shows, mostly in Utah and California. His current interest in furniture is "to combine art and daily life. If there is a contradiction here, I prefer to leave the question to the semantics people and art historians."

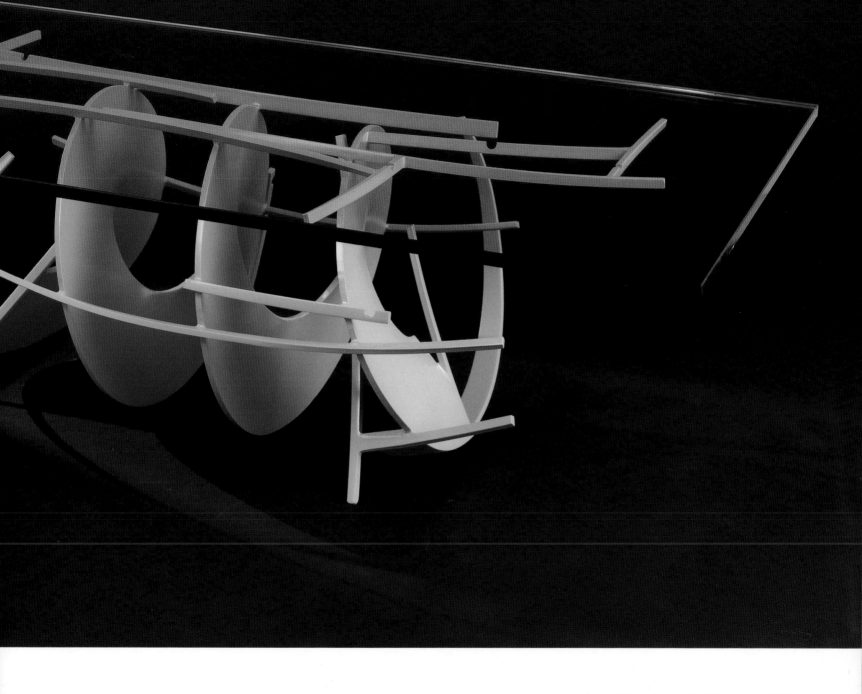

FURNI

ROSANNE SOMERSON

■ Her exquisite craftsmanship and high-style design have attracted an enthusiastic audience of collectors and gallerygoers, and her influence as acting head of the Graduate Furniture Program at the Rhode Island School of Design (RISD) has earned her a special prominence in contemporary woodworking. Formerly an editor of *Fine Woodworking* magazine, Rosanne Somerson is also an outspoken commentator on her field and the ironies with which it is now faced.

"On the one hand, furniture makers are getting more publicity then ever before. The good ones have work backed up two to three years, and client interest is in-creasing all the time," observes Somerson. "On the other hand, economics are forcing the graduate [woodworking] schools to shut down program space; there are no craft programs in the high schools; and it is difficult to earn a living making one-of-a-kind pieces because the best talents con-centrate in metropolitan areas where

Woodworker Rosanne Somerson in Westport, Massachusetts, studio that she shares with her husband, furniture artist Alphonse Mattia. OPPOSITE Close-up of high-backed chair commissioned in 1988 for office reception area. Chair is bubinga and solid Macassar ebony with silk upholstery.

TURE

Evolution of commissioned chair from early drawings to finished product illustrates Somerson's process. "It's important to me to draw all the time. Sometimes the subconscious puts things down on the page that make sense later and inspire the best work." *BELOW LEFT* Studio assistant Joshua Goldberg at work on high-backed chair. Carefully labeled inventory of woods *OPPOSITE* stored overhead in common machine room that Somerson and Mattia share—her inventory on the left, his on the right. Like the inventory, individual "bench rooms," or studios, are separated by partitions.

space is expensive and galleries fail at an alarming rate."

In part, Somerson attributes this dilemma to the dramatic shift in cultural values that has taken place in the United States over the last twenty years. "In the fifties and sixties, it was easier to be an artist. Most of the people who are successful woodworkers today grew up in a counterculture environment where making money was not thought to be the most important thing in life." Now, according to Somerson, "people coming out of craft schools have to be much tougher than we were: They have to face the Yuppie culture of the eighties and the fact that they are considered failures if they don't earn $100,000 a year by the time they're thirty."

Somerson's concerns are born out by the program that she, herself, heads: Although the largest in the country and at an all-time high enrollment, the RISD Graduate Furniture Program produced only eight M.F.A.'s in 1989. Moreover, many of today's graduates are somewhat older people looking for more creative career paths. "The average entry age in woodworking is not twenty-one," says Somerson, "it's twenty-six. And many of these people go into architectural woodworking or small contract design studios—rather than one-of-a-kind furniture making—because business is booming there."

The drift of trained woodworkers to more lucrative commercial jobs is part of what Somerson sees as a much larger problem. "The movement right now is being dispersed; it's wiggling in and out of

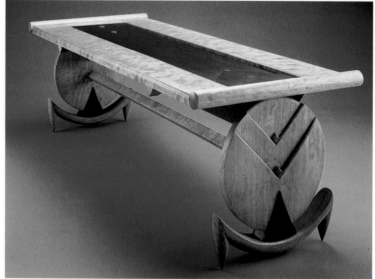

art and architecture as well as production design, and there is no common agenda." Her proposed solution is more government support for the American craft movement (à la Great Britain's Craft Council) and a stronger SOFA (Society of Furniture Artists), an organization she helped to establish in 1988.

Despite this hardheaded assessment of the woodworking field today, Somerson is tremendously gratified by her own role in it. While teaching two days a week and caring for her infant daughter, Isabel, she produces a steady output of one-of-a-kind

ABOVE LEFT TO RIGHT
Upholstered bench, pearwood, bleached
curly maple, and leather, 1986;
"High-Heeled Table," cherry, ebony, and
glass, 1984; conference table, bubinga, maple,
glass, and anodized aluminum, 1983; and
reading couch, bleached white oak and Thai
silk, 1987. OPPOSITE BELOW Somerson's
sideboard in bleached wenge and white oak
with botocino marble top, 1988.

and limited-production furniture on both commission and speculation. "I make furniture that fuses function with ornament. . . . I try to draw the viewer in with pleasing overall form and a hint of mystery . . . then I try to hold the viewer by layering my work with levels of detail that cause the eye to explore components of the piece. Sometimes, I include forms that suggest associations, hoping to engage the viewer's sense of imagery."

Somerson's emphasis on the visual aspects of her work may be the result of an early interest in photography, her major when she entered RISD in 1971 after spending a year in Denmark as a photographer. Soon frustrated by the two-dimensional nature of the medium, she switched to a woodworking class taught by renowned Danish-born instructor Tage Frid, who promptly dubbed her "ten thumbs." Undaunted, she went on to win a summer scholarship to Scotland, where she apprenticed as a cooper in a distillery.

where she apprenticed as a cooper in a distillery.

Graduating from RISD with a B.F.A. in industrial design in 1976, she started writing for *Fine Woodworking,* taught woodworking to public-school children grades K through 8, then sublet space at the Cambridgeport (Massachusetts) Cooperative Workshops, where founding member Judy Kensley McKie and other prominent furniture artists maintain their studios to this day. Finally, in 1979, Somerson and furniture artist Alphonse Mattia (pages 214 to 215), whom she met while a freshman at RISD and later married, set up shop in an old Boston farmhouse with attached barn.

"When you looked out the window, all you saw were trees, though if you could see past them, you'd probably spot kids ripping the radio out of your car." Eight years later, Somerson and Mattia moved to Westport, Massachusetts, where they now share a huge studio in the midst of a pasture. "We haven't lost a car radio yet."

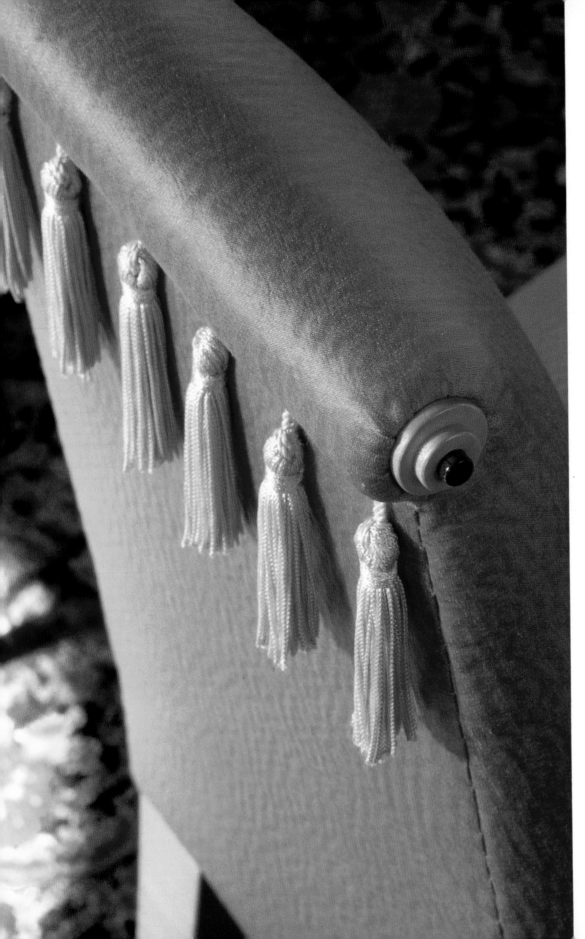

JOHN DUNNIGAN

Best known for his frankly luxurious chairs and sofas, John Dunnigan is one of a growing number of woodworkers who are turning their attention to upholstered furniture. For Dunnigan, the allure of upholstery is rooted in the concept of comfort. "It's not enough that a chair is comfortable—comfort is visual, too. A chair should *look* inviting and make people feel good while they sit in it."

Dunnigan, who in 1980 completed an M.F.A. in furniture design at the Rhode Island School of Design (RISD), where he now teaches, has been designing and making furniture since 1975, when he established John Dunnigan and Co. in West Kingston, Rhode Island. In 1986, he formed a partnership with Wendy Wahl (Dunnigan Wahl Associates, Saunderstown, Rhode Island) that specializes in designing carpets such as those installed in the Joseph apartment (pages 64 to 77). The Joseph apartment also chronicles a recent expansion of Dunnigan's design interests beyond furniture, rugs, and upholstery fabric to lighting, textiles, table linens, and architectural glass—a contemporary recall of the Arts and Crafts ideal of unified interiors.

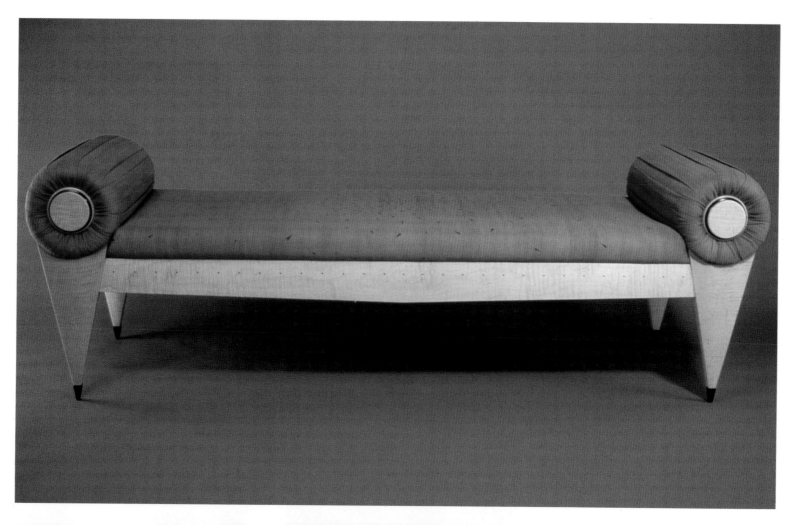

Dunnigan's classically inspired daybed ABOVE is upholstered in pink silk over maple frame, 1986. Table LEFT is bird's-eye maple with inlaid top of French Deco linoleum, 1988. Chair DETAIL OPPOSITE is maple and rosewood upholstered in silk with silk tassel trim, 1986.

WENDY MARUYAMA

■ Regarded as one of the foremost West Coast furniture artists, Wendy Maruyama has been designing and making furniture since 1975. Best known early in her career for bold, colorful architecturally inspired designs, Maruyama's interests have recently shifted to more organic, free-form shapes and pure, furniture-related forms. "I find that doing these two types of work keeps me well rounded, mentally, that each inspires me to do the other (surprisingly). I'm intrigued with the idea of combining organic shape with the typically nonorganic format in architectural designs."

Maruyama, who now works out of a studio in Berkeley, completed an M.F.A. in 1980 at the Rochester Institute of Technology. Prior to that, she studied furniture

making at Boston University and is currently head of the woodworking and furniture-design program at the California College of Arts and Crafts in Oakland. Over the last ten years, her work has appeared in more than forty major exhibitions around the country, including several one-woman shows. A frequent lecturer, Maruyama has been published extensively and is represented in numerous private collections, including the Abramson, Bennett, Choi, and Coady residences.

OPPOSITE LEFT is Maruyama's "Urban Amazon" hat rack; carved and polychromed basswood, 1987. Her "Primitive Bench with Yellow Snakes" DETAIL LEFT is also carved and polychromed basswood, 1988. ABOVE Bleached mahogany credenza commissioned by Paul and Gloria Choi (pages 32 to 39), 1988.

ALPHONSE MATTIA

With no arts background, Alphonse Mattia left a Catholic high school and headed straight for the clearest alternative available: Pennsylvania College of Art. "My father was an Italian carpenter with aspirations for his son to rise above 'hand work,' so I enrolled in the least 'arty' program I could find—industrial design. Then one day, I wandered into the woodworking studio and something went 'snap': I knew what I wanted to do with my life."

Earning his way through college as an occupational therapist in woodworking at the University of Pennsylvania, Mattia went on to the Rhode Island School of Design (RISD), where he studied with Tage Frid, the Danish cabinetmaker and teacher whose career is regarded as a seminal force in contemporary American woodworking. In 1973, with an M.F.A. in industrial design, he went directly into teaching ("that made my father very happy").

Since 1985, he has been head of the woodworking and furniture-design studio at the Swain School of Design, now incorporated into Southeastern Massachusetts College of Fine and Performing Arts—a

career that has not slowed Mattia's output from the Westport, Massachusetts, studio that he shares with his wife, furniture maker Rosanne Somerson (pages 204 to 209). Best known for his limited editions of witty sculptural valets, Mattia is represented in the American Crafts Museum, Yale University Art Gallery, Boston Museum of Fine Arts, and RISD Museum, as well as numerous private collections.

Alphonse Mattia's blanket chest ABOVE is padouk, pearwood, and purpleheart with aromatic cedar, 1988. RIGHT Bird's-eye maple and painted birch ply valet, 1986, one of several limited-edition designs in which he reinterprets this traditional furniture type as an art form with obvious anthropomorphic references (see also pages 63 and 103). Head of this valet opens to reveal mirror DETAIL OPPOSITE.

JAMES SCHRIBER

James Schriber's lacewood bench with Macasser ebony stretchers and "buttons" has leather upholstered bolsters strapped to frame, 1989. Sleigh bed ABOVE RIGHT is solid cherry, figured cherry veneer, and Macasser ebony, 1988. BELOW Schriber's thirty-six-inch round table of purpleheart, 1982.

Ohio-born furniture maker James Schriber left his home state to do undergraduate studies at Goddard College in Vermont, then attended Philadelphia College of Art and, in 1979, received his Certificate of Mastery from Boston University's renowned Program in Artisanry. He now works out of a studio in New Milford, Connecticut—a pattern of migration to New England that many contemporary craft artists have followed.

An independent designer and fabricator since 1980, Schriber has undertaken several corporate commissions, including the executive offices of L. M. Dalton and MONY Financial Services. He is also represented in the private collections of Ronald and Anne Abramson, Pat and Judy Coady, and Bernice Wollman/Warren Rubin, for whom he recently completed an entire suite of bedroom furniture (see page 125). Recently Schriber has taught at the California College of Arts and Crafts in Oakland and the Swain School of Design in New Bedford.

THOMAS HUCKER

■ One of the few craft artists recognized to date by mass-production designers, Thomas Hucker has twice been cited in *Industrial Design* magazine's prestigious Annual Design Reviews (1987 and 1988). The artistic range and technical mastery of Hucker's work reflect, in part, an unusual training.

Beginning in 1974 as a private student of Philadelphia furniture maker Leonard Hilgner (a fifth-generation German traditional craftsman), Hucker went on to study at the Ura Sanke School of Japanese Tea Ceremony, Boston Chapter. In 1980, he received a Certificate of Mastery in Furniture Design and Fabrication from Boston University and, in 1982, was an artist-in-residence at Tokyo University of Fine Arts. In 1988, Hucker was awarded a Fulbright-Hays Scholarship to study and travel in Italy, and during 1989 resided in Milan as a student at Domus Academy.

When not traveling, teaching, or studying abroad, Hucker works out of his studio in Charlestown, Massachusetts, producing highly sophisticated designs in which the Japanese influence often dominates. Represented in the permanent collection of the Boston Museum of Fine Arts, Hucker's pieces also appear in major private collections such as that of Anne and Ron Abramson in Washington, D.C.

*Hucker's dining table for three LEFT, DETAIL
ABOVE, is Carpathian elm burl and beefwood,
1988. Low table OPPOSITE is beefwood
and bronze, 1982, and is housed in the Asian
wing of the Boston Museum of Fine Arts.*

Timothy Philbrick's "Grecian Sofa," 1985, is curly maple with silk upholstered down cushion. Night table OPPOSITE is pearwood and maple, 1988.

TIMOTHY PHILBRICK

Working out of a turn-of-the-century carriage house in Narragansett, Rhode Island, that was once part of his great-grandparents's oceanfront estate, Tim Philbrick has been designing and making furniture since 1978, when he was graduated from Boston University's Program in Artisanry with a certificate of mastery in wood furniture design. Prior to that, he had run an antiques store in California, and from 1971 to 1975 was apprenticed to a Rhode Island restorer and reproducer of American period furniture.

"I believe that pleasing proportion—the relation of one part to another—is central to good furniture design," says Philbrick. "I strive to create furniture that is graceful, balanced, and sensuous . . . to give each piece a clear, quietly stylish stance . . . to select woods that complement the overall feel of a piece and grain patterns that enhance the curve or shape of an individual part." Philbrick, who has been commissioned for the permanent collections of the Boston Museum of Fine Arts and the Rhode Island School of Design Museum, is represented in numerous private collections throughout the United States.

RICHARD SCOTT NEWMAN

Richard Scott Newman's ten-foot demilune console ABOVE, made in 1986, is Swiss pearwood and ebony with bronze appliqués and faces made by Jennifer Beckley DETAIL OPPOSITE. RIGHT Small demilune console and mirror. Console is mahogany and ebony with vermeil appliqué DETAIL LOWER RIGHT, 1987. Mirror is framed in mahogany and ebony, 1988.

The refinement of Richard Scott Newman's neoclassical designs make this craft artist's work especially appealing to corporate commissioners, private collectors, and institutions who value the tradition of fine furniture making. Elegant details, such as the fluting, twisting, and gilded rosettes that are Newman's hallmark, give his pieces an opulence reminiscent of Louis XVI and Empire furniture, but at a much lighter, more delicate scale.

An undergraduate student of engineering physics at Cornell University, Newman received a B.F.A. in woodworking and furniture design from the Rochester Institute of Technology's School for American Craftsmen in 1974. In 1979 he taught banjo-making there, a discipline to which he attributes the extraordinary detailing of the furniture he has been making since 1969. Represented in the Boston Museum of Fine Arts, Abramson, and Joseph collections, Newman also has pieces installed in the headquarters of the Coca-Cola, Gannett, and Kellogg corporations. He works out of a studio in Rochester, New York, where from 1982 to 1984 he was on the faculty of the Wendell Castle Workshop.

WENDY STAYMAN

A furniture maker since 1981, Wendy Stayman began her career with a B.A. in art history from the University of Pennsylvania, apprenticed herself to a cabinetmaker/furniture restorer, then became a museum restorationist and earned her master's degree in art conservation at Queen's University, Ontario. After four more years as a museum conservator, she enrolled in the Wendell Castle School (now incorporated into Rochester Institute of Technology) with the idea of spending a year there refining her restoration skills. Instead, Stayman's studies evolved into a full program of furniture making, from which she was graduated in 1983, staying on another year as artist-in-residence at the renowned Castle school.

Recently much acclaimed for her crisp, architecturally based designs and finely tuned woodworking techniques, Stayman had her first show only eight years ago: "Women Are Woodworking," The Gallery at Workbench, 1982. She is currently working out of a studio in Easthampton, Massachusetts, where she designs and makes furniture on speculation as well as for corporate and private commissions.

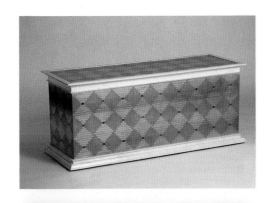

Small round side table OPPOSITE is one of a series that Wendy Stayman has designed and made since 1987. This one has a curly maple base and black bean top with ebony inlay. ABOVE Curly maple and holly writing table with silver and slate drawer pull, 1987. Cedar chest CENTER is scribed and painted curly maple, 1984. The desk LEFT is steamed Swiss pearwood, holly, and curly maple with silver and brass pull, 1983.

225

BRUCE VOLZ

■ Born in Minnesota, Bruce Volz received a B.A. in social sciences and early-childhood development from St. John's University in Collegeville before moving east to the Leeds Design Workshop in Easthampton, Massachusetts, where he earned his M.A. in 1980. An instructor in woodworking at the Wendell Castle School from 1980 until 1982 and, after that, at Leeds, Volz has settled in Easthampton, where he maintains his studio. He has been an independent woodworker since 1983, designing and making furniture on both a commissioned and speculative basis.

Volz's work ranges from meticulous inlay and marquetry to fresh, seemingly hurried finishes such as the painted table shown here. Represented in the Joseph, Abramson, and MONY Financial Services collections, Volz has recently undertaken two residential commissions with architect Robert A. M. Stern, for whom he has made dining room furniture based on Stern's designs. Widely exhibited, Volz's work has appeared at the Pritam & Eames Gallery in Easthampton, New York; the Elements Gallery in Greenwich, Connecticut; and the Snyderman Gallery in Philadelphia.

Bruce Volz's "Vanishing Species" table
ABOVE, DETAIL OPPOSITE, is painted
cherry, glass, Plexiglas, and lucite, 1988.
"Peter's T.V. Table" CENTER is bleached
maple, dyed maple, ebony, and gold leaf, 1987;
small round side table TOP RIGHT is ebonized
walnut and bleached birch, 1986. RIGHT Side
cabinet of bleached maple and dyed bird's-eye
veneer with a marble top and brass pulls, 1987.

MICHAEL HURWITZ

"I respond to a certain quality in ancient and primitive art which I perceive as originating from genuine creative necessity. Efforts born out of this need reflect an honesty and directness that I don't always see in work resulting from more deliberate action." The primitive quality of which Michael Hurwitz speaks is evident in much of this Philadelphia craft artist's own work, which has been featured in more than sixty exhibitions over the last ten years, mostly on the East Coast.

A 1975 graduate of Boston University's Program in Artisanry, Hurwitz is now assistant professor in the wood program at the University of the Arts, Philadelphia, and has lectured and conducted workshops in such far-flung places as the Tokyo School of Art (1988) and Altos de Chavón, Dominican Republic (1985). Along with twenty-five other second-generation furniture makers (i.e., craft artists who began working around 1975 or later), Hurwitz is represented in the Boston Museum of Fine Arts's 1989 exhibition "New American Furniture." Of his work, Hurwitz says, "I try to be sensitive to the nature of wood, allowing it to help determine the form and content that ultimately emerge," an attitude that has carried forward from such first-generation woodworkers as James Krenov, Sam Maloof, and George Nakashima. He is represented in a number of major private collections, including the Abramson, Coady, and Joseph residences.

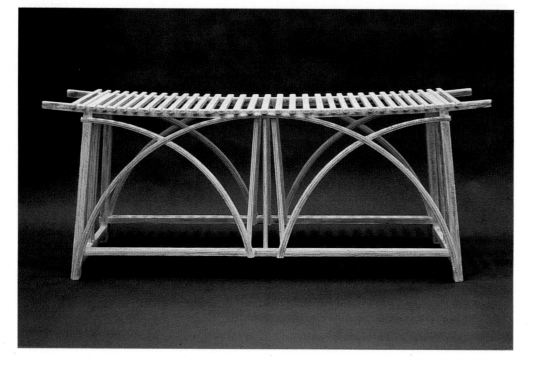

Michael Hurwitz's bench with slatted seat LEFT is wenge, 1986. The tall table OPPOSITE is cherry, 1982.

PETER DEAN

Peter Dean's first job out of high school was as an architectural model maker, an occupation that soon led him back to night school at the Boston Architectural Center, then on to a B.F.A. in architecture from the Rhode Island School of Design (RISD). After graduate work in theology and psychology at the University of Notre Dame, Dean returned to design via a sculpture workshop at Indiana University, eventually to be graduated from Boston University's Program in Artisanry (1984). Since 1985, he has been working out of his Charlestown, Massachusetts, studio, designing furniture that clearly reveals his early architectural training.

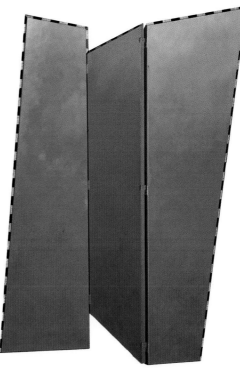

Peter Dean's "Pharaoh's Table" CENTER is holly, ebony, cherry, gold leaf, and watercolor lacquer with glass top inset, 1988. FAR LEFT "Ariel" chair, with lacquered mahogany frame, ash seat frame, and birch panels covered by upholstery. Colorcore and spruce "Landscape" screen ABOVE appeared in final installation of Formica Corporation's three-year traveling exhibition "Surface and Ornament," Cincinnati, 1986.

THOMAS LOESER

A graduate of Boston University's Program in Artisanry, Tom Loeser has been designing and building furniture since 1982. For several years he worked out of the Cambridgeport (Massachusetts) Cooperative Workshop, an old industrial space shared by fourteen craft artists, including Judy Kensley McKie (pages 234 to 239), Mitch Ryerson (pages 248 to 249), and Michael Pierschalla (page 105). Then, in 1989, Loeser moved his studio to the West Coast, where he now teaches at the California College of Arts and Crafts.

Not the first in his family to make a career in contemporary craft (his mother, Herta Loeser, is past president and a lifetime trustee of the Society of Arts and Crafts in Boston), Loeser has developed a distinctive style of furniture making that combines simple geometric form with elaborately painted surfaces, often in brightly contrasting pastel colors. His work has appeared in more than forty exhibitions, including "Post Modern Colour: New Furniture by British, American and French Designers" at the Victoria and Albert Museum (London, 1984), and he is represented in the permanent collection of the Cooper-Hewitt Museum, New York City. Loeser is also among the twenty-six artists represented in the Boston Museum of Fine Arts "New American Furniture" show now touring the United States.

Tom Loeser has produced numerous versions of this ingenious folding chair, each in different combinations of materials, finish treatments, and color patterns. Version shown here is Baltic birch plywood, enamel, and steel, 1984.

JUDY KENSLEY McKIE

"Actually, I'm not a great animal lover," confesses Judy Kensley McKie. "I started making straightforward furniture and wanted to animate it, so I sat in front of a traditional piece and stared until its structure was transformed. What I saw was a four-legged animal." And what has flowed from McKie's studio since is some of the most creative design in contemporary woodworking—all of it shaped in or embellished with animal forms: not ordinary zoological specimens, but twisted, turning, elongated creatures with wicked grins and knowing eyes whose nearest relatives last appeared in medieval bestiaries.

"I was always fascinated with primitive, stylized animal shapes," McKie explains, "and after a while it became an obsession." That obsession is matched by an insatiable appetite for the hard work of furniture making, the techniques of which she has taught herself through endless hours of trial and error. Sometimes, she has "invented" or improvised a technique, only to learn later that it was used 150 years ago by Pennsylvania German cabinetmakers. Once, having lent a kitchen

McKie's carved wood lizard serves as door pull
OPPOSITE at 16 Emily Street, the famous
Cambridgeport [Massachusetts] Cooperative
Workshops TOP RIGHT where she shares space
with thirteen other woodworkers. Inside, the
front of this old industrial building LEFT is
used as common storage area for wood inventory
and large tools. Around the common space are
individual workshops such as the one in which
McKie ABOVE trades grins with one of two
panthers that will be positioned back to front so
that they can grip a glass tabletop in their teeth.
Made in 1988 of laminated, carved, stained,
and painted mahogany, these same shapes were
cast in a limited edition of bronzes in 1989.
McKie's interest in casting was inspired by West
Coast furniture maker Garry Knox Bennett
who, convinced that her animal shapes were
ideal for casting, introduced her to the Oakland
foundry where she continues to have all her
bronze work done.

Blanket chest ABOVE AND RIGHT is McKie's work in progress for the Boston Museum of Fine Arts "New American Furniture" exhibition, 1989. Like each of the other twenty-four pieces commissioned for that show, it references an historical piece from the museum's permanent collection—in this instance, a chest by Charles Prendergast. Beginning with small sketches enlarged by an opaque projector, McKie has traced the leopard pattern on the four sides and top (inside as well) of the chest, then carved it in low relief prior to gilding, antiquing, and painting. Although she sometimes hires up to three assistants when things are busy, McKie prefers to do all work herself. "It's the drawing that takes the longest time, and because it's such an important part of the process, I like to show it with the finished piece."

table to a chain-smoking friend who returned it with cigarette burns, she noted that the intense black centers of the burns, with their hazy outlines, were just the spots she wanted for a leopard couch then in construction. So she burned the spots in with a propane torch.

This ability to "feel her way through" the design process—the thing that gives McKie's work its unique emotional charge—may be, in part, the result of never formally having studied furniture making. Graduated in 1966 from the Rhode Island School of Design (RISD) with a B.F.A. in painting, she taught school for a year, then made appliquéd banners and wall hangings with her husband, artist Todd McKie. (Some of their giant banners at the Woodstock festival were torn down and used as tents when it started to rain on that historic gathering.) For seven or eight years, she also built furniture—simple, utilitarian pieces for her own apartment and those of her friends. Then one day, she began to make small boxes with fanciful animals carved in low relief, pieces that her husband liked so much that he gave her a woodworker's canvas tool roll for Christmas, along with a gift certificate to fill it.

That was in 1975, when many of the second-generation woodworkers had just begun to emerge, but at the time McKie knew nothing about them, their work, or the movement in which she and they were shortly to be joined. In fact, her first "serious" furniture was not too different from the plywood cabinets that preceded it, except that it was more consciously designed

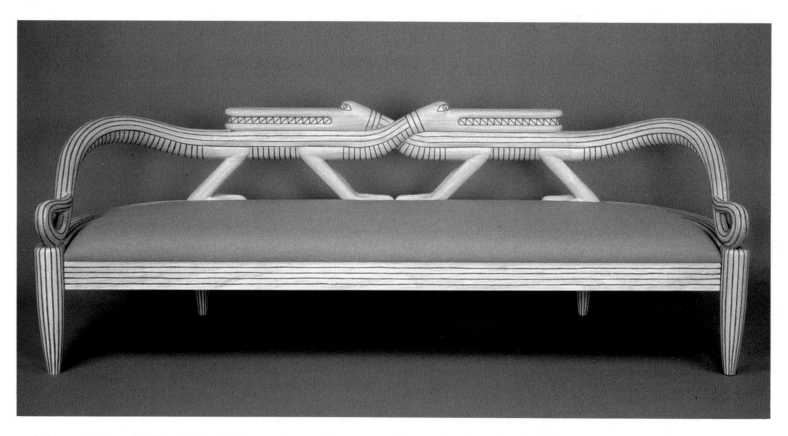

and decoratively embellished. Gradually, by learning how to integrate various woodworking techniques into the making of one piece, McKie evolved the intriguing, dynamic style that, today, makes her one of the most critically acclaimed and widely popular furniture artists in America.

The work that has earned McKie this prominence was first exposed to the public in "New Handmade Furniture," an exhibition mounted by the American Craft Museum in 1979, the same year that the Boston Museum of Fine Arts commissioned her to make a bench for its permanent collection. An instant success, artistically, McKie has since been showcased in more than sixty major museum and gallery shows; has won two National Endowment for the Arts Craftsman's Fellowships, a Massachusetts Artists Foundation Fellowship, and a Certificate of Design Excellence; and is represented in most of the important private collections in the United States. Nevertheless, earning a living as a woodworker has not been any easier for McKie than it is for most craft artists.

Until about five years ago, when her furniture began to command prices commensurate with her reputation, the difference between time and materials required to produce a piece and the amount of money for which it could be sold was so marginal that, but for a timely and generous foundation grant, McKie would have had to take out a bank loan to finance the year it took to prepare for her first New York City gallery show. Now, with knowledgeable dealers to set fair prices and negotiate commissions for them, McKie and other successful woodworkers are enjoying strong demand and growing recognition of the true worth of their talents. The fear remains, however, that gallery markups and rising costs of work space could put art/craft furniture beyond the reach of many clients who supported the movement in its formative years. Only recently, McKie and the thirteen other woodworkers with whom she shares space in the Cambridgeport Cooperative Workshops (founded 1973) won a costly two-year legal battle against

eviction proceedings that could have wiped out their careers.

In many respects, McKie's evolution as a woodworker chronicles the contemporary art/craft movement itself: beginning in the late sixties when making (mostly primitive) things by hand was fashionable; rapidly becoming more sophisticated under the influence of graduate programs, where the emphasis shifted from industrial design to a more personal, open-ended process; and now appreciated by an audience that, by and large, did not even exist twenty years ago. "Of course," says McKie, "being in it, I hardly think about the movement as such. I just do what I do because I really love it."

"Chase Table," made in 1987, is one of an edition of eight and McKie's first cast bronze work. Her "Lizard Couch" OPPOSITE is carved, bleached, and burned mahogany, 1987. The bird plant stand CENTER, carved and painted poplar, is one of an edition of ten that she made in 1982.

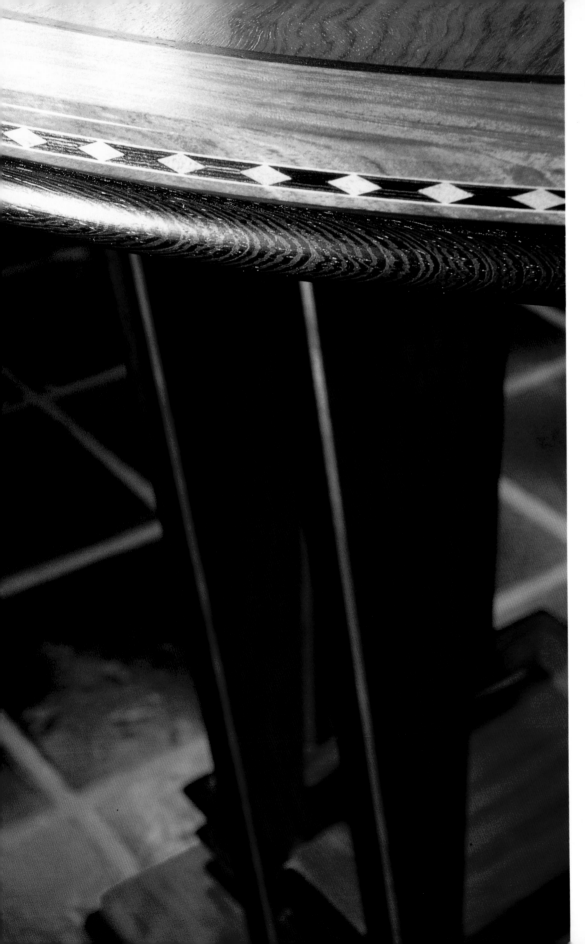

RONALD PUCKETT

"Some of my pieces have a definite architectural look and feel," Ron Puckett acknowledges—the legacy of his early studies in architecture at Virginia Polytechnic Institute. From VPI, Puckett went on to receive a B.F.A. from Virginia Commonwealth University, then trained as a furniture maker at the Rhode Island School of Design (RISD), where he completed an M.F.A. in 1977 and spent another year as assistant to Tage Frid, the influential Danish-born cabinetmaker and teacher who was professor of woodworking at RISD from 1962 until his retirement in 1985.

The way in which architectural sensibilities and fine woodworking technique combine—each carefully respected yet so completely joined that neither is aesthetically subordinated to the other—is the potent force in Puckett's work. An independent craft artist from 1978 to 1987, Puckett is now vice-president of operations and design at The Wayne Guild, Inc., in Richmond, Virginia. Although not teaching at present, he has been an adjunct faculty member in the crafts department at Virginia Commonwealth University (1980) and continues to lecture and give workshops.

Ron Puckett's "Tobacco Heir" side cabinet DETAIL ABOVE is stained maple, padouk, and lacewood, 1984. Tall "William Morris" liquor cabinet NEAR LEFT is bubinga, pearwood, and wenge, 1985. Round table FAR LEFT, DETAIL OPPOSITE is bubinga and wenge, 1987. Table and cabinets reveal Puckett's architectural leanings, yet all three pieces are distinguished by fine woodworking so evident in side cabinet detail.

GAIL FREDELL SMITH

Another of the younger West Coast furniture artists whose work has been gaining prominence nationally and abroad, Gail Fredell Smith was trained as an architect at the University of California, Berkeley. For four years she practiced as a partner in a small Oakland building design and contracting firm, then enrolled at Rochester Institute of Technology where, in 1980, she received an M.F.A. in woodworking and furniture design. Since 1980, Smith has maintained a studio in Oakland, designing and making both commissioned and speculative pieces.

Currently an instructor in woodworking and furniture design at California College of Arts and Crafts, Oakland, Smith describes her work as "architectural in nature: compositions of hard-edged geometric forms, assembled in a somewhat constructivist manner, employing contrasting elements of natural wood, painted surfaces, and metal. Engineering structure, building materials, and machinery components provide various points of departure." Smith's work has been exhibited in more than twenty-five shows over the last ten years, mostly in California.

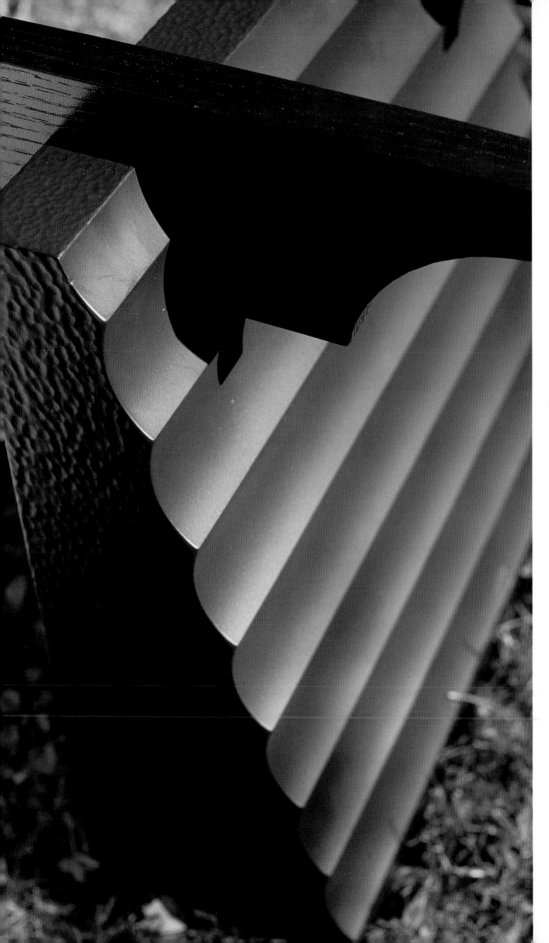

Gail Fredell Smith's bench (bleached lacewood, lacquered oak, and maple, 1987) is characterized by an apparent simplicity inspired, she says, "by an affinity for the minimalism of modern art and design, and by the Zen aesthetic of understatement and restraint. The goal of this aesthetic is to achieve a sense of resolution and internal harmony . . . by creating an interdependent relationship among various . . . elements of form, detail, and material. All contribute to the whole, and none can be removed without lessening the impact of the statement."

JACK LARIMORE

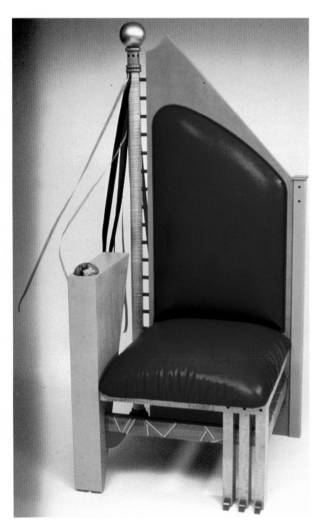

Born in Illinois and educated in land-scape architecture at Michigan State University, Jack Larimore quickly became disillusioned with the constraints imposed by large-scale projects, so he took a leave of absence and renovated an old row house in Philadelphia. "I found myself enjoying that process so much that I went on to carpentry, then zeroed in on furniture making."

The turning point in Larimore's career was his exposure to Richard Kagan's former gallery on Philadelphia's South Street, one of the first in this country to specialize in wood and furniture. "The things I saw there influenced me tremendously, and I started making pieces on speculation. Nobody paid much attention until I got into the Philadelphia Craft Show. Then the galleries were excited, and I started receiving commissions."

Jack Larimore's "Chair's Chair," made for the 1984 exhibition "Material Evidence," is Colorcore, curly maple, Honduras mahogany, ebony, leather, lacquer paint, gilding, silk ribbon, and electric components. His "Impatient" hall table RIGHT is polychromed medium-density fiberboard, Colorcore, and mother-of-pearl, 1987.

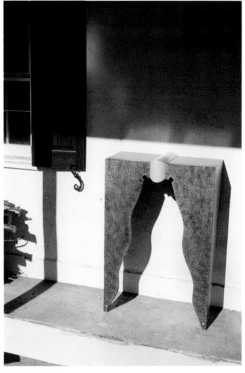

In 1984, Larimore was one of nineteen artists commissioned by The Gallery at Workbench to design furniture using Colorcore, a then-revolutionary Formica product in which color is present throughout the plastic laminate rather than just on the surface. The chair that Larimore produced for this landmark exhibition ("Material Evidence") reveals the Art Deco edge to his work, a tendency that Larimore himself downplays. "I'm not interested in Art Deco style per se, but there is in my work a sense of humor—of humanity, really—and an eclecticism and use of color that has much in common with the Art Deco impulse. What I retain of my original training in landscape architecture is the connection to design and design process, and particularly to the commissioning process."

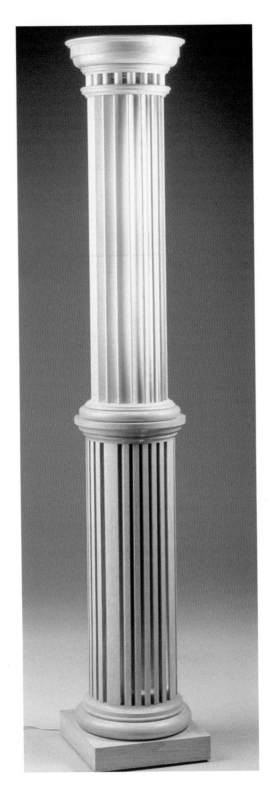

PETER SPADONE

One of the more recently emerged talents in contemporary furniture making, Peter Spadone began his career designing and producing vacuum-formed cedar canoes, then went on to architectural woodworking, custom kitchens, and independent cabinetmaking. In 1981, he returned to school, earning a B.F.A. in furniture design from Boston University's Program in Artisanry.

Since 1984, Spadone has been designing and making furniture out of a studio in Kennebunk, Maine, where he recently formed a partnership with former Boston University classmate Stephen Rieger. (Rieger, prior to joining Spadone, worked for three years in Alphonse Mattia's studio, pages 214 and 215.) Together, Spadone and Rieger have expanded the Kennebunk studio to handle larger commissions and limited production runs, the design for which reflects Spadone's interest in layering traditional architectural and furniture forms with his own ideas about the vocabulary of contemporary craft. Represented in the MONY collection, Spadone has also been exhibited at the Society of Arts and Crafts in Boston and other East Coast galleries.

Peter Spadone's lady's writing desk BELOW, DETAIL OPPOSITE, is amaranth and maple with ebony pulls, 1988. FAR RIGHT TOP His partner Stephen Rieger's high-backed chair of walnut upholstered in wool, 1987; FAR RIGHT BOTTOM Adjustable easel in amaranth, maple, ebony, and brass, 1987. Spadone/Rieger's light column, 1987 LEFT, is a seventy-seven-inch-high classically inspired column of bleached white oak with "fluting" of open vertical slats through which incandescent light is visible.

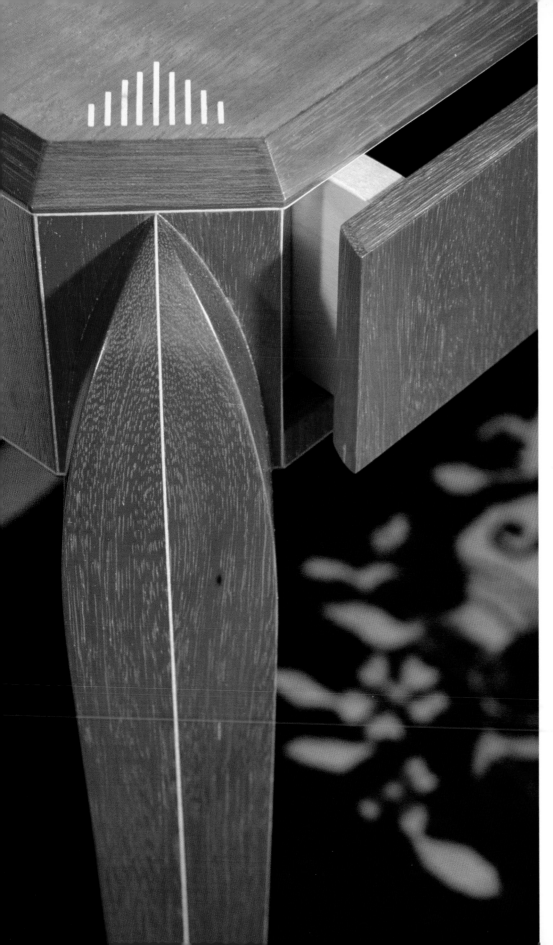

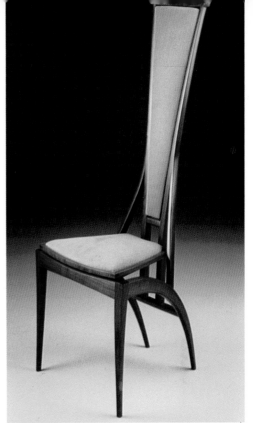

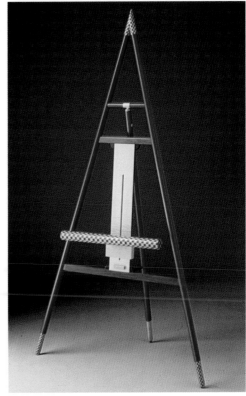

MITCH RYERSON

"When I create a new piece [of furniture], it is often influenced by something similar that I have lived with or have imagined living with. I use color, playful arrangement . . . and anything else I can think of to make furniture that I hope is irresistibly inviting and reasonably functional." For Mitch Ryerson, an unabashed eclectic who rummages his own subconscious as freely as he references the history of design, the words *reasonably functional* are key: While most of his pieces are usable, Ryerson's primary purpose in furniture making is self-expression.

A meticulous craftsman, Ryerson was a boat builder in Maine when he became interested in the comparative design freedom of furniture making and returned to his native Boston to earn a B.F.A. at Boston University's much-acclaimed Program in Artisanry. Since 1982, he has been working out of the Cambridgeport Cooperative Workshops, along with Judy Kensley McKie, Tom Loeser, Michael Pierschalla, and ten other furniture artists. Ryerson also teaches, formerly at the Swain School of Design, New Bedford, and the Penland School of Crafts, North Carolina.

Mitch Ryerson's "Wheel Chair" ABOVE is polychromed maple, 1983. His "Elizabethan Cabinet" LEFT is maple, plywood, basswood, mahogany, and wrought iron with lacquer and oil glaze finishes, 1988.
OPPOSITE LEFT Ryerson's "Farmboy Chest"; polychromed maple with produce shipping box labels, 1984. "Washboard High Chair" FAR RIGHT is curly maple and cherry with a washboard, soap-box labels, clothespins, and lacquer finishes, 1986.

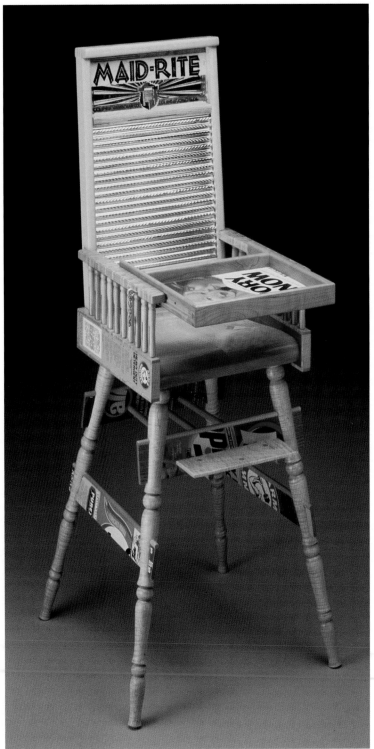

KRISTINA MADSEN

■ In the ten years that she has been woodworking, Kristina Madsen has attracted collectors and corporate commissioners who, like Madsen herself, are interested in the visual enrichment of interior space through the exquisite detailing of fine furniture. Trained at the Leeds Design Workshop in Easthampton, Massachusetts, Madsen was the 1988 artist-in-residence at the University of Tasmania School of Art in Hobart, the principal city of the Australian island that supplies the world with some of its most exotic woods.

Madsen's talents, which earned her a National Endowment for the Arts Craftsman's Fellowship in 1980–1981, have also attracted prestigious commissions from clients such as the Chubb Corporation, for which she designed and made an executive dining table, chairs, and sideboards in 1984. She currently works out of a studio in Easthampton, Massachusetts, and is represented in the permanent collection of the Brockton Art Museum, and the Abramson collection in Washington, D.C. Madsen also exhibits at a number of East Coast galleries, including Snyderman, Pritam & Eames, and Henoch.

Kristina Madsen's sumptuously upholstered bench is wenge with silk moiré cushions and two loose bolsters, 1988. Feathers that "stand proud" in silk tassels attached to wenge bolster buttons reveal Madsen's fascination with the detail of fine furniture.

GARRY KNOX BENNETT

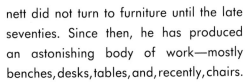

At six foot seven, with a girth that attests to a near-legendary love of food and drink, Garry Knox Bennett is the Paul Bunyan of contemporary craft furniture—larger than life in spirit as well as physical presence. A student of metal sculpture at the California College of Arts and Crafts in the fifties and maker of roach clips and peace symbols in the sixties, Bennett did not turn to furniture until the late seventies. Since then, he has produced an astonishing body of work—mostly benches, desks, tables, and, recently, chairs.

Entirely self-taught, Bennett likes to work in wood because "it's a rapid medium to make fairly large objects . . . I'm not into tricky joinery. . . . I just want to do something the best fastest way—not the best slowest and not the worst fastest—the best fastest. . . . The thing I enjoy is when a piece is really good and I can say, 'Goddamn, boy, that came right out of the old gourd real quick . . . booma-booma-booma.'"

When the natural color or grain of a wood appeals to him, Bennett will incorporate it into a design, but he has no compunction about painting wood or "arting up" mistakes. He also mixes woods with glass, aluminum, copper, brass, and plastic laminate—in audacious combinations that Rick Snyderman (owner of the Snyderman Gallery) describes as "clearly American. Extroverted, full of energy. Exaggerated in scale yet carefully balanced with discrete and intimate detail." Like Bennett himself.

Garry Knox Bennett's 1988 trestle table OPPOSITE TOP is natural and ebonized walnut and burnished aluminum with glass top cut in a squiggle painted bright red. "This curvy line," observes gallery owner Rick Snyderman, "a signature detail in much of his work, is Bennett's visual way of giving an Oakland 'raspberry' to cold, slick, hard-edged Eurodesign and its American counterparts." OPPOSITE BELOW A game table and four chairs in claro walnut, leather, Macassar ebony, glass, metal, wood beads, and copper rivets, 1989.

WENDELL CASTLE

■ No discussion of contemporary woodworking could be complete without reference to Wendell Castle, whose thirty-year career has overlapped the first and second generations of postwar furniture making. He began teaching and working in the early 1960s, and the biomorphic pieces he produced through the mid-1970s had more to do with the oeuvre of Esherick, et al. than with the new wave of art furniture then emerging. Nonetheless, Castle leapt to the forefront of contemporary woodworking when, in the late 1970s, he switched from carved, laminated solid forms to more traditional stick-and-board furniture.

By the early 1980s Castle had not only embraced many of the ideas being explored by the second generation, he had eclipsed them, taking furniture making to the limits of craftsmanship in his Art Deco-inspired "Fountain Cabinet"; appropriating architectural post-modernism in his "Hall Table"; and producing thirteen startlingly anthropomorphic tall clocks sold for prices four to ten times higher than the market for handmade furniture at the time. Since then, Castle's furniture has become

In his Scottsville, New York, studio, Wendell Castle spends a good deal of time drawing, sometimes making as many as three hundred sketches for a single piece of furniture. To help in the building of his designs (each of his tall clock cases required four to six thousand work hours), Castle employs up to fifteen shop assistants at any one time, usually furniture makers in their own right and many trained by Castle himself. Each assistant is assigned a project that he or she sees through from beginning to end, but Castle (shown here making the base for cabinet) does all the design work and keeps a hand in every project.

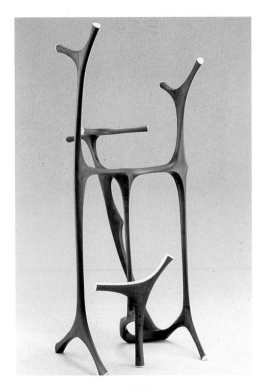

256 *Art for Everyday*

Of Castle's recent work, critic Lisa Hammel has said:

"Castle is now making nonfurniture. He is treating wood as if it were rubber, metal, or clay. . . . The newer pieces play with space and gravity . . . defying the laws of balance in nature. . . . Ultimately, he believes in a balance of opposites—negative and positive space, beauty balanced by what he calls 'necessary ugliness.' He sees in aesthetics an extended and uneasy symmetry, with logic at its center."

OPPOSITE TOP, LEFT TO RIGHT "Stool Sculpture," walnut and ivory, 1958–1959; walnut "Library Sculpture" incorporating stool, desk light, and two connecting chairs, 1965; "Benny Light," glass-reinforced polyester and neon, 1969. BOTTOM, LEFT TO RIGHT "Coat on a Chair," maple, 1978; "Fountain" cabinet, English walnut with silver inlay, 1982; "Sun God" clock, tulipwood, purpleheart, rosewood, gold-plated cast-bronze birds, gold leaf on wood, and metal, 1985. TOP RIGHT "Atlantis" desk; ebonized and lacquered cherry, beeswing narra veneer, plastic, and silver-plated brass, 1982. BOTTOM RIGHT "Never Complain, Never Explain" table; poplar, purpleheart, holly veneer, leather, gold-plated copper rings, and plastic, 1985.

ABOVE LEFT "Old Number 107"; stained curly maple veneer, ebony veneer, and ebonized cherry, 1986. ABOVE RIGHT "Tree Farming in Babylon," stained curly maple veneer, ebony veneer, ebonized mahogany, solid maple, and rubber, 1986. LEFT "Common Ground"; cherry, patinated copper, lacewood veneer, and Plexiglas, 1989. OPPOSITE "Cavalcade," poplar, bleached lacewood, patinated copper, gold leaf, and mahogany, 1989.

increasingly expressive and less functional, leaving his audience to wonder what he can possibly do next without moving into the realm of pure sculpture.

Such a move would bring Castle's career full cycle, back to his early training at the University of Kansas where, in 1958, he received a B.F.A. in industrial design, then an M.F.A. in sculpture. Almost immediately upon graduation, he found himself teaching furniture making at the Rochester Institute of Technology (RIT) School for American Craftsmen, one of the most important centers of contemporary woodworking in this country. In 1980, he formed the Wendell Castle School in his own Scottsville, New York, studio. There, until 1988 when it was absorbed into RIT, more than a hundred furniture makers were trained, several of whom, like Wendy Stayman, have become prominent among second-generation woodworkers.

Today Castle's work can be seen not only in institutions well known for their contemporary furniture collections but in the Metropolitan Museum of Art, the Museum of Modern Art, the Chicago Art Institute, and the Philadelphia Art Museum. And although few can afford the prices that his work now commands, most private buyers do not consider their collections complete without a Castle piece.

Unquestionably the foremost furniture maker in America today, Wendell Castle has pushed craftsmanship—and with it public appreciation for craftsmanship—further than anyone thirty years ago could have dreamed was possible.

DIRECTORY OF CRAFT GALLERIES AND ORGANIZATIONS

The following is a selected listing, by geographical region, of galleries that regularly show handmade furniture and/or architecturally scaled glass, metalwork, and ceramics. Not included are the museums and numerous commercial galleries that mount occasional exhibitions, information about which can be obtained from one of the national craft organizations also listed here.

MID-ATLANTIC

Art and Architecture
1112 St. Paul
Baltimore, MD 21202
(301) 837-1112

Lewis Dolin
588 Broadway
New York, NY 10012
(212) 941-8130

Helen Drutt Gallery
724 Fifth Avenue
New York, NY 10019
(212) 974-7700

Garth Clark Gallery
24 West 57th Street
New York, NY 10019
(212) 246-2205

Charles Cowles Gallery
420 West Broadway
New York, NY 10012
(212) 925-3500

Craftsman's Gallery
16 Chase Road
Scarsdale, NY 10583
(914) 725-4644

Barbara Fendrick Gallery
568 Broadway
New York, NY 10012
(212) 226-3881

The Fendrick Gallery
3059 M Street NW
Washington, DC 20007
(202) 338-4544

Gallery of Applied Arts
24 West 57th Street
New York, NY 10019
(212) 765-3560

Heller Gallery
71 Greene Street
New York, NY 10021
(212) 966-5948

Henoch Gallery
80 Wooster Street
New York, NY 10012
(212) 966-0303

Hudson River Gallery
217 Main Street
Ossining, NY 10562
(914) 762-5300

Meredith Gallery
805 North Charles Street
Baltimore, MD 21201
(301) 873-3575

Dennis Miller Associates
19 West 21st Street
New York, NY 10010
(212) 242-7842

Alexander Milliken Gallery
98 Prince Street
New York, NY 10021
(212) 966-7800

Sheila Nussbaum Gallery
358 Millburn Avenue
Millburn, NJ 07041
(201) 467-1720

Franklin Parrasch Gallery
2114 R Street NW
Washington, DC 20008
(202) 328-8222/4554
and
584 Broadway
New York, NY 10012
(212) 925-7090

Pritam & Eames
29 Race Lane
East Hampton, NY 11937
(516) 324-7111

Max Protech Gallery
560 Broadway
New York, NY 10012
(212) 966-5454

Snyderman Gallery
317 South Street
Philadelphia, PA 19147
(215) 238-9576

Bernice Steinbaum Gallery
132 Greene Street
New York, NY 10012
(212) 431-4224

Swan Gallery
132 South 18th Street
Philadelphia, PA 19118
(215) 542-0218

The Works Gallery
319 South Street
Phildelphia, PA 19147
(215) 922-7775

MIDWEST

Craft Alliance Gallery
6640 Delmar
St. Louis, MO 63130
(314) 725-1151

The Dairy Barn
P.O. Box 747
Athens, OH 45701
(614) 592-7253

Habatat Gallery
32255 Northwestern Highway
Farmington Hills, MI 48018
(313) 851-9090

Hokin/Kaufman Gallery
210 West Superior
Chicago, IL 60610
(312) 266-1211

Katie Gringrass Gallery
714 North Milwaukee Street
Milwaukee, WI 53202
(414) 289-0855

Betsy Rosenfeld Gallery
212 West Superior
Chicago, IL 60610
(312) 787-8020

Esther Saks Gallery
311 West Superior
Chicago, IL 60610
(312) 751-0911

Yaw Gallery
550 North Woodward
Birmingham, MI 48009
(313) 747-5470

NEW ENGLAND

Artsource
10 Bay Street, Suite 58
Westport, CT 06880
(203) 222-9264

Brookfield Craft Center
P.O. Box 122, Route 25
Brookfield, CT 06804
(203) 775-4526

Clark Gallery
Box 339, Lincoln Station
Lincoln, MA 01773
(617) 259-8303

The Elements
14 Liberty Way
Greenwich, CT 06830
(203) 661-0014

Mendelson Gallery
Titus Square
Washington Depot, CT 06794
(203) 868-0307

Gallery NAGA
67 Newbury Street
Boston, MA 02116
(617) 267-9060

The Signatures Gallery
One Dock Square
North Street
Boston, MA 02109
(617) 227-4885

The Silo Gallery
44 Upland Road
New Milford, CT 06776
(203) 355-0300

The Society of Arts and Crafts
175 Newbury Street
Boston, MA 02116
(617) 266-1810

SOUTHEAST

Axis 20
22-B East Andrews Drive NW
Atlanta, GA 30305
(404) 261-4022

Fay Gold Gallery
247 Buckhead Avenue
Atlanta, GA 30305
(404) 233-3843

Eve Manes Gallery
116 Bennett Street
Atlanta, GA 30309
(404) 351-6651

Habatat Gallery
608 Banyan Trail
Boca Raton, FL 33431
(407) 241-4544

SOUTHWEST

Carr Gallery
1827 Branard
Houston, TX 77098
(713) 520-0187

Janne Rapp/The Hand in
the Spirit Gallery
4200 North Marshall Way
Scottsdale, AZ 85251
(602) 949-1262

Yuma Art Center
281 Gila Street
Yuma, AZ 85364
(602) 783-2314

WEST COAST

Artworks Gallery
155 South Main Street
Seattle, WA 98104
(206) 625-0932

Agnes Bourne, Inc.
Showplace Square West
550 Fifteenth Street, #34
San Francisco, CA 94103
(415) 626-6883

Virginia Breier Gallery
3091 Sacramento Street
San Francisco, CA 94115
(415) 929-7173

Susan Cummings Gallery
32 Miller Avenue
Mill Valley, CA 94941
(415) 383-1512

Garth Clark Gallery
5820 Wilshire Boulevard
Los Angeles, CA 90036
(213) 939-2189

Contemporary Crafts Gallery
3934 SW Corbett Avenue
Portland, OR 97201
(503) 223-2659

Fine Woodworking
1201 Bridgeway
Sausalito, CA 94965
(415) 332-5770

Frank & Dunya
3418 Fremont Avenue North
Seattle, WA 98103
(206) 547-6760

Gallery 8
7464 Gireard Avenue
La Jolla, CA 92037
(619) 454-9781

Gallery Fair
Box 263
Mendocino, CA 95460
(707) 937-5121

Highlight Gallery
P.O. Box 1515
Mendocino, CA 95460
(707) 937-3132

Northwest Gallery of Fine
Woodworking
202 First Avenue South
Seattle, WA 98104
(206) 625-0542 and
317 NW Gilman Boulevard
Issaquah, WA 98027
(206) 391-4221

Paul-Luster Gallery
336 Hayes Street
San Francisco, CA 94102
(415) 431-8511

Walter Gallery
1001 Colorado Avenue
Santa Monica, CA 90401
(213) 395-1155

NATIONAL CRAFT
ORGANIZATIONS

American Craft Council
40 East 53rd Street
New York, NY 10019
(212) 956-3535

Artist-Blacksmiths' Association of
North America (ABANA)
P.O. Box 1181
Nashville, TN 47448
(812) 988-6919

Glass Art Society
P.O. Box 1364
Corning, NY 14830
(217) 469-2436

Society of Furniture Artists (SOFA)
P.O. Box 416, Kendall Square
Cambridge, MA 02142
(617) 636-5918

Woodworking Association of
North America
P.O. Box 706, Route # 3
Plymouth, NH 03264
(603) 536-3876

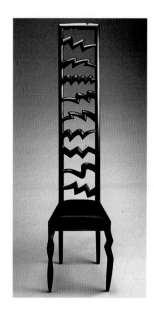

INDEX

Aalto, Alvar, 140–141
Aberdeen, The, 176
Abramson, Anne and
    Ronald, 26, 94–107,
    213, 217, 218, 223, 226,
    228, 250
Aesthetic movement, 10–12,
    15
Alaska Performing Arts
    Center, 145, 148–149
Albany, N.Y. state capitol
    building gates (Paley),
    192
American Craft Council, 104,
    177
American Craft Enterprises,
    177
American Craft Museum, 23,
    164, 215, 238
Anchorage Performing Arts
    Center, 145, 148–149
architecture and craft,
    136–157
Armstrong, Tom, 189
Arneson, Robert, 42
    "Funny Vace," 42
Art Deco, 18, 138, 145, 150,
    163, 245
Art Nouveau, 15–16, 191
Arts and Craft movement,
    10–16, 19, 23
Ashbee, Charles Robert, 13
Ashbee, Janet, 13
Associated Artists, 10, 12
Attwood, James, 138,
    140–141

Bakst, Marni, 168–171
    La Delice, lighted wall for,
    168
    "Rainbow Wall," 168
Barbara Fendrick Gallery,
    40
Barker, Warren, 185

Barnes, Edward Larabee,
    146
Bauhaus, 19
Bean, Bennett, 51
Beckley, Jennifer, 223
Beeken, Bruce, 51
Bennett, Garry Knox, 35, 36,
    39, 60, 91, 92, 110, 111,
    122, 127–135, 213, 235,
    252–253
    "African" chair, 127
    "Bow-Wow, Cluck-Cluck"
        bench, 62
    "Cabinet with Lights," 131
    "Checkerboard" bench, 88
    "Cloud" floor lamp, 135
    "Nail" cabinet, 131, 133
    "Noguchi on Sticks"
        bench, 128
Bennett, Sylvia, 127, 130, 133
Boston Museum of Fine Arts,
    189, 215, 218, 219, 221,
    223, 228, 232, 236, 238
Boston University, 20, 213,
    217, 218, 221, 228, 230,
    246, 248
Brandt, Edgar, 82
Brockton Art Museum, 250
Broholm, Dale, 108, 110
Broom, Oringdulph, O'Toole
    and Rudolph, Architects,
    176
Butterfield, Deborah, 42

California College of Arts
    and Crafts, 168, 213,
    217, 232, 242, 252
Cambridgeport Cooperative
    Workshops, 209, 232,
    238, 248
Carnegie-Mellon Institute,
    189

Carpenter, Arthur Espenet,
    19, 22, 130, 132
    "Captain's Chair," 22
    "Wishbone" chair, 132
Carpenter, Ed, 145, 148–149,
    174–177
    "Labyrinth" mosaic
        panels, 149
Carpenter, James, 146
Castle, Wendell, 20–22, 30,
    32, 36, 40, 42, 53, 67, 68,
    71–75, 78, 93, 95, 96,
    127, 130, 254–259
    "Atlantis" desk, 257
    "Benny Light," 257
    "Caligari" library wall, 71
    "Cavalcade," 258
    "Cloth Without Table," 42
    "Coat on a Chair," 257
    "Common Ground," 258
    "Crescent" rocker, 83, 85
    "Fountain" cabinet, 254, 257
    "Four Years Before Lunch:
        Grandson in Hawaiian
        Shirt," 55
    "Hall Table," 254
    "He Came Without His
        Wallet" cabinet, 29
    "Library Sculpture," 257
    "Magician's Birthday"
        clock, 54
    "Midnight Marriage, The"
        hall table, 99
    "Molar" chairs and table,
        35, 38, 55
    "Never Complain, Never
        Explain" table, 257
    "Old Number 107," 258
    "Plantain" coffee table,
        64, 69
    "Stool Sculpture," 257
    "Sub-Nine" table, 29, 69
    "Sun God" clock, 257
    "Table with Gloves and
        Keys," 53, 54
    "Temple Desk and Chair,"
        53, 54
    "Three-Columned Table,"
        131
    "Three-Legged" side
        chairs, 78, 85
    "Tree Farming in
        Babylon," 258
    "Umbrella Stand with
        Umbrella," 72
Wendell Castle School, 225,
    226, 259
Cedarquist, John, 102
Central Park Zoo gate
    proposal (Paley), 194
Chapel of St. Frances
    Cabrini, 168

Chicago Art Institute, 259
Chihuly, Dale, 142–145, 144
Choi, Gloria and Paul, 32–
    39, 213
Christian Theological
    Seminary, 146–147
Coady, Judy and Pat, 60–63,
    108, 122, 171, 213, 217,
    228
Colman, Samuel, 12
Cooper-Hewitt Museum, 232
Cooper Square Site I
    Housing Development,
    168
Corbin house, 11
Corning Museum of Glass,
    164
Cosma, Christopher, 83
Cosmopolitan Apartments,
    163, 164
Craftsman, The, 14, 16
Cranbrook Academy of Art,
    19, 139, 202
Cranbrook style, 19, 138
Crowley, Charles, 95

Dailey, Dan, 95, 96, 142,
    143, 144, 145
    "Etrus" tripods, 96
    "Orbit" wall, 142, 143, 144
L. M. Dalton, 217
David M. Schwarz
    Architectural Services,
    26, 30, 67, 99
Davidt, Carl Andree, 108,
    110
    "Green Cloud Caution
        Marker" lamp, 108
Dean, Peter, 96, 230–231
    "Ariel" chair, 231
    "Landscape" screen, 231
    "Pharoah's Table," 231
DeForest, Lockwood, 12
Del Guidici, Mark, 104, 106
directory of craft galleries
    and organizations, 260–
    261
Dunnigan, John, 47, 56, 59,
    64, 68, 71, 72, 75, 96,
    104, 210–211
    "Biedermeier Suite," 64
    "Entasis" torchers, 64
    "Golden Section" rug, 72
    "Jewel" rug, 64
    "Jungle" rug, 75
    "Metamorphosis" series,
        64
    "Tardis" chairs, 75
    "WJ" rug, 71
John Dunnigan and Co., 210

Ebner, David, 44, 104
Elements Gallery, 226
Ellis, Harvey, 14
Embassy Row house, 26–31
Esherick, Wharton, 19, 60,
    254

Farley, Richard, 140
Fauset, Kalle, 106
    "Moon" chair, 106
Fendrick, Barbara, 40–43
Barbara Fendrick Gallery,
    40
Fendrick Gallery, The, 40
Figliuzzi, Teri, 140
Fine Woodworking, 205, 209
Formica Corporation, 231,
    245
Frid, Tage, 20, 209, 214, 240
Furness, Frank, 12
furniture, 204–259

Galleries, directory of, 260–
    261
Gallery at Workbench, The,
    60, 108, 122–125, 153,
    225, 245
Gamble house, 14
Gerakaris, Dimitri, 125
Gerner, Randolph, 154
Gilpin, Hank, 47, 48, 118
Glaser, Milton, 142, 163
glass, 160–177
Glass Art Society, 167
Goldberg, Joshua, 206
Gordon, George, 47
Graves, Michael, 93
Greene, Charles Sumner, 14,
    15, 16
Greene, Henry Mather, 14,
    15, 16
Greenland Studio, 168
Griggs Lee Rutt Architects,
    174

Hall, Marsha, 164
Hammel, Lisa, 257
Hardy, Hugh, 142, 145, 163
Hardy Holzman Pfeiffer
    Associates, 142, 145,
    148, 177
Hawke, Ted, 44
Heller, Eugene and Sheila,
    56–59
Henoch Gallery, 250
Henson, Jim, 78–85
Hilgner, Leonard, 218
Hill House, 13
Hoffman, Josef, 12, 15, 16,
    154, 157
    "Villa Gallia" armchairs,
        154, 157

Home Box Office
    headquarters, 136, 150–
    153
Hubbard, Elbert, 12, 16
Hucker, Thomas, 102, 218–
    219
Hunter-Stiebel, Penelope,
    191
Hurwitz, Michael, 96, 114,
    117, 228–229

Industrial Design, 218
International Ceramic
    Museum, 189

Jackson, Dakota, 93
Jackson, Dan, 20
John Dunnigan and Co., 210
Johnson, Bebe and Warren,
    44–51, 65
Johnston, Richard, 202
Joseph, Peter, 26, 64–77,
    210, 223, 226, 228
    "Judy Said, 'Time's Up!' "
    table, 158
Justice Center, Portland,
    Ore., 176

Kagan, Richard, 244
Kahn, John, 81, 83
Kaiser Permanente Medical
    Center, 176
Keyser, Howard, 200
King, Ray, 144, 145, 161–165
    "Saturn" table lights, 144,
    145
Kingscote, 9, 10
Klimt, Gustav, 12
Kopf, Silas, 32
Krenov, James, 20, 21, 47,
    48, 114, 117, 118, 120,
    228
    "Walkaround" cabinet, 21
Kronick, Richard, 138

Larimore, Jack, 24, 62, 91,
    150, 153, 244–245
    "Chair's Chair," 244
    "Impatient" hall table, 244
Larsen, Jack Lenor, 47, 48,
    67, 99, 101
Leavitt, Greg and Lydia,
    197–199
    "Delphinium" gate, 198
    "Peacock" gate, 198
    Upper Bank Nursery
    "Delphinium" gate, 198
Leeds Design Workshop,
    226, 250
Leslie, Constance, 158, 179–
    185

Lethaby, W. R., 13
Lewis, Andy and Ginny, 24,
    90–93
Lewis, Frances, 91
Lewis, Sidney, 91–92
L. M. Dalton, 217
Loeser, Herta, 232
Loeser, Tom, 95, 232–233,
    248
Loos, Adolf, 15

MacDonald, Elizabeth, 125,
    186–187
Mack, Ben, 56
McKie, Judy Kensley, 60, 68,
    83–85, 93, 118, 120, 130,
    131, 132, 209, 232, 234–
    239, 248
    "Bird Table," 64
    "Carved Bird" cabinet, 75,
    77
    "Chase" table, 71, 127,
    133, 239
    "Dog Eat Dog" table, 56,
    59, 123
    "Dragonfly" chest of
    drawers, 77
    "Jungle" dining table and
    chairs, 59, 78, 81, 82, 83
    "Lizard Couch," 239
    "Lizard" plant stand, 82,
    85
    "Snake" plant stand, 88
    "Snake" table, 49, 127
    "Table with Grinning
    Beasts," 75
    "Turtle" bench, 78, 82, 85
    "Turtle" bowl, 82
McKie, Todd, 236
Mackintosh, Charles Rennie,
    13, 14, 15, 16
Mackmurdo, A. H., 13
McNaughton, John, 158
Madsen, Kristina, 123,
    250–251
Makepeace, John, 19, 21, 93,
    102
    "Espalier" dining chairs,
    21
Maloof, Sam, 19, 21, 30, 82,
    85, 228
Mandelbaum, Ellen, 172–173
    "Roberta Window," 172
Manning, Anne, 83, 154–157
Manuel, K. Lee, 36, 127, 131
Marble Collegiate Church,
    168
March, Robert, 67
Mark, Charles, 101
Mark Saw Chain
    headquarters, 174
Maruyama, Wendy, 35, 39,

130, 132, 212–213
    "Mickey Mackintosh"
    chair, 35, 132
    "Primitive Bench with
    Yellow Snakes," 213
    "Urban Amazon" hat rack,
    213
"Material Evidence"
    exhibition, 245
Mattia, Alphonse, 62, 102,
    104, 205, 206, 209, 214–
    215, 246
    "Architect's Valet," 102
    "City Boy" valet, 62
    "Knothead" valet, 102
    "Mr. Potato-Head" valet,
    102
metal, 190–203
Metropolitan Museum of Art,
    189, 259
Meyer May house, 15, 16
Milliken, Alexander
    "Sandy," 52–55
Milliken, Bettina, 53
Modern movement, 10
MONY Financial Services
    headquarters, 136, 138–
    141, 217, 226, 246
Morris, Marshall, Faulkner &
    Co., 13
Morris, William, 13–15, 16
Moss, Vickie, 96
Museum of Modern Art, 259
Myers, Forest, 93

Nakashima, George, 19, 22,
    228
    "Conoid" chair, 22
National Cathedral, 200
Neidecken, George Mann,
    15, 16
"New American Furniture"
    exhibition, 228, 232, 236
"New Handmade Furniture"
    exhibition, 238
Newman, Richard Scott, 44,
    68, 69, 75, 222–223
    "Dream" chair, 69
Norvell, Patsy, 78, 81, 83

O'Neil, Tim, 176
Oregon School of Arts and
    Crafts, 177
organizations, directory of,
    260–261
Osgood, Jere, 20, 21, 56,
    60, 62, 75, 113, 114,
    116–117
Ozgrow, Beth, 182, 185

Paley, Albert, 40, 42, 53, 54,
    75, 145, 191–195
    Marriott Hotel gates, 192
    Renwick Gallery gates,
    191, 192
Panaitescu, Ruxandra, 138
Pandick, Inc. executive
    offices, 154–157
Penland School of Crafts,
    248
Pennsylvania College of Art,
    214
Perceval, Brian, 172
Petersen, Norman, 35, 36,
    39, 127, 130, 133, 135
    "Ball and Cone" chair, 127
Philadelphia Art Museum,
    259
Philadelphia College of Art
    (PCA), 20, 217
Philbrick, Timothy, 44, 75,
    140, 220–221
    "Grecian Sofa," 220
Pierobon, Peter, 96
    "Madonna" tall clock, 96
Pierschalla, Michael, 104,
    232, 248
Pilchuck Glass Center, 167
Piper, John, 177
Post Modernism, 23
Prendergast, Charles, 236
Pritam & Eames Gallery, 44,
    65, 118, 226, 250
Program in Artisanry (PIA) at
    Boston University, 20,
    217, 221, 228, 230, 246,
    248
Puckett, Ronald, 31, 47, 51,
    106, 140, 240–241
    "Tobacco Heir" side
    cabinet, 241
    "William Morris" liquor
    cabinet, 241
Pugin, A. W. N., 13

Quagliata, Narcissus, 93,
    166

Radenkov, Zivko, 114, 117
    "Winter" cabinet, 114
Rainbow Room, 142–145,
    161, 163
Ray, Christopher, 197, 200
    "Wissahickon Valley"
    gate, 200
Renwick Gallery, 104
Reyntiens, Patrick, 177
Rhode Island School of
    Design (RISD), 20, 167,
    179, 205, 207, 209, 210,
    214, 230, 236, 240

Rhode Island School of
    Design Museum, 215,
    221
Rieger, Stephen, 246
Riley, Brigette, 127
Rochester Institute of
    Technology (RIT), 20,
    193, 212, 223, 225,
    242, 259
Rockefeller Center Rainbow
    Room, 142–145, 161,
    163
Rose, Laura, 183, 184
Roycrofters Community, 12–
    13, 16
Rubin, Warren, 60, 122–125,
    186, 217
Ruhlmann, Jacques-Emile, 29
Ruskin, John, 13, 16
Ryerson, Mitch, 232,
    248–249
    "Elizabethan Cabinet,"
    248
    "Farmboy Chest," 248
    "Washboard High Chair,"
    248
    "Wheel Chair," 248

Saarinen, Eliel, 18, 19, 139,
    140
Schaffrath, Ludwig, 177
School for American
    Craftsmen (SAC) at
    Rochester Institute of
    Technology, 20, 223
Schriber, James, 29, 30, 48,
    60, 104, 124, 125, 140,
    216–217
Schwarz, David, 26–30, 101
David M. Schwarz
    Architectural Services,
    26, 30, 67, 99
Scott, M. H. Baillie, 13, 14
Seawright, Jim, 68
Sheemas, Joanne, 110, 111
Simpson, Tommy, 123, 128,
    130, 133
    "Boxer's Chair," 128, 133
    "Howdy House Before"
    cabinet, 123
Skywa-Primavesi house, 12
Smith, Gail Fredell, 36, 39,
    242–243
Snyderman, Rick, 108, 252
Snyderman, Ruth, 108
Snyderman Gallery, 108,
    226, 250, 252
Society of Arts and Crafts,
    232, 246
SOFA (Society of Furniture
    Artists), 209
Somerson, Rosanne, 49, 96,
    104, 108, 205–209, 215

"Earring" cabinet and mirror, 104
"High-Heeled Table," 209
"Radiator" coffee table, 96
Sottsass, Ettore, 93
Southern Massachusetts College of Fine and Performing Arts, 214–215
Spadone, Peter, 139, 140, 246–247
S. S. White Building, 163
Stained Glass School, The, 172
Stanger, Jay, 96, 99
Starke, Philipe, 31
Stayman, Wendy, 69, 71, 85, 113, 117, 138, 139, 140, 224–225, 259
Stern, Robert A. M., 226
Stickley, Gustav, 14, 16
Stinsmuehlen-Amend, Susan, 166–167
"Arched Post" door panel, 167
"Diagonal with Del" leaded glass door, 167
Stoclet house, 12
Strickland, Ken, 111
Sullivan, Louis, 12, 16
"Surface and Ornament" exhibition, 231
Swain School of Design, 214–215, 217, 248
Swanson, Judy, 150

Tarver, Catharine, 140
Taylor, Adina, 172
Taylor-Hewlett, 176
Temple University, Tyler School of Art at, 191
Tiffany, Louis Comfort, 10, 12, 16, 85
tile, 178–189
Tokyo School of Art, 228
Tokyo University of Fine Arts, 218
Tracy, Joseph, 49
Trotman, Bob, 24, 93
"Dancing" end tables, 93
Tsirantonakis, Anthony, 78, 83, 150, 153
Tyler School of Art at Temple University, 191

University of the Arts, 228

Valcarcel, Miguel, 138
Vallin, Eugène, 11
Venturi, Robert, 93

Victoria and Albert Museum, 164, 189, 232
Volz, Bruce, 26, 29, 69, 72, 75, 138, 139, 226–227
"American Flyer I" cabinet, 69, 72
"American Flyer II" cabinet, 29
"Peter's T.V. Table," 227
"Vanishing Species" table, 227
Voysey, C. F. A., 13

Wahl, Wendy, 64, 71, 72, 75, 210
"Golden Section" rug, 72
"Jewel" rug, 64
"WJ" rug, 71
Warner, Geoffrey, 113, 117
Wasserman & Waterhouse, 172
Wayne Guild, Inc., The, 240
Webb, Philip, 13
Wegner, Hans, 118
Wendell Castle School, 225, 226, 259
Wheeler, Candace, 12
Whistler, James Abbott McNeill, 12
White, Stanford, 10
S. S. White Building, 163
Whitley, Robert, 9, 24, 86–88, 91
"Throne Chair," 9
Whitney, Steven, 26
Whittelsey, Steven, 87, 88
Wollman, Bernice, 60, 122–125, 186, 217
"Women Are Woodworking" exhibition, 122, 225
Woodman, Betty, 188–189
"Window with Flower Boxes," 189
Wright, Frank Lloyd, 15, 16, 141
Wrigley, Rick, 136, 153, 154, 156, 157

Yale University Art Gallery, 215

Zimmer Gunsul Frasca, 176, 177
Zucca, Ed, 60, 91, 92, 96, 99, 101, 124, 125
"Time is Money" tall clock, 96, 99

PHOTOGRAPH CREDITS

All photographs in this book are under copyright protection and, except as noted below, are by Jon Jensen.